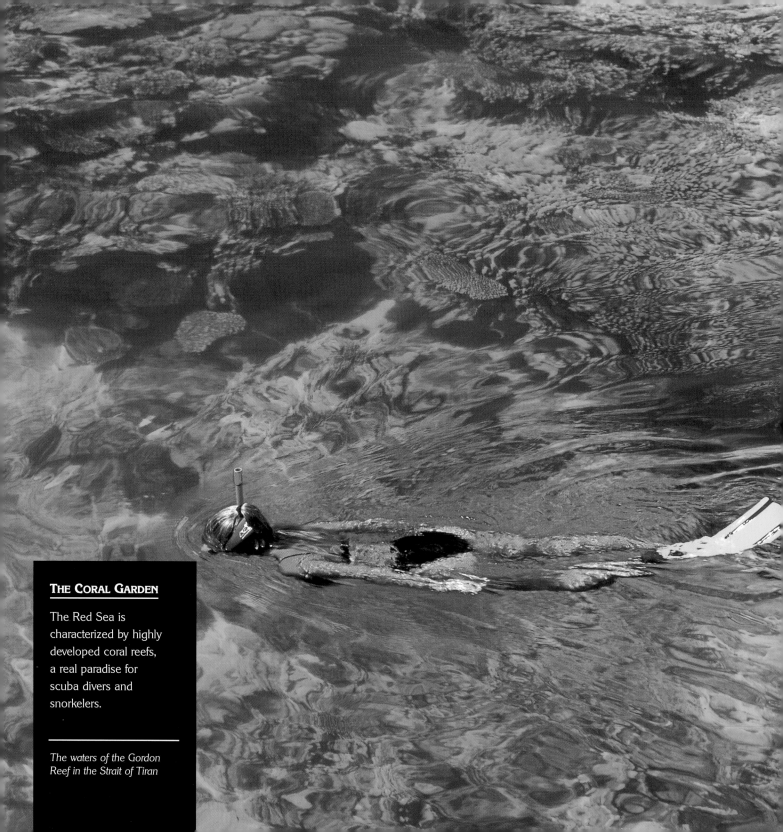

THE CORAL GARDEN

The Red Sea is characterized by highly developed coral reefs, a real paradise for scuba divers and snorkelers.

The waters of the Gordon Reef in the Strait of Tiran

THE RED SEA
The Coral Garden

ALBERTO SILIOTTI

GEODIA EDIZIONI

THE UNDERWATER GARDEN

The development of
coral reefs in the
Red Sea is due to
climatic conditions that
are extremely favorable
to the growth of coral
polyps.

*Madrepore formations to the
south-west of Ras Mohammed*

AN EXTRAORDINARY WORLD

The coral reef constitutes a complex ecosystem in which hundreds of different genera and species coexist.

The coral reef in the Hurghada area

Text Alberto Siliotti

Photographs Franco Banfi, Claudio Bertasini, Manfred Bortoli, Claudio Cangini, Arnaud Chicurel, Jack Janson, Laurence Lagny, Silvia Liotta, Patrick Lousy, Martina Milanese, Nasa, Vincenzo Paolillo, Daniele Pellegrini, Alberto Siliotti, Egidio Trainito

Drawings Stefania Cossu, Stefano Trainito

General Editing Yvonne Marzoni

ISBN(13) 978-88-87177-55-8   ISBN(8)   88-87177-55-4
Dar el-Kotub 2004/3791

Printed in Egypt

In the photo: the thin graceful branches of whip coral (Juncella juncea) a member of the family Gorgonacea, rise toward the surface.

Contents

A forest of Gorgonians (Subergorgia hicksoni)

The Red Sea anemonefish (Amphiprion bicinctus)

A pair of dolphins (Tursiops truncatus)

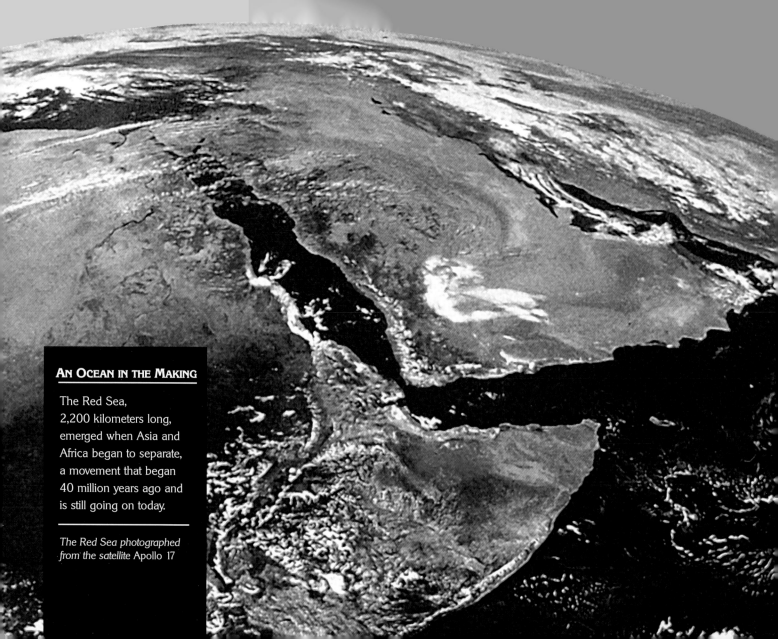

AN OCEAN IN THE MAKING

The Red Sea,
2,200 kilometers long,
emerged when Asia and
Africa began to separate,
a movement that began
40 million years ago and
is still going on today.

*The Red Sea photographed
from the satellite Apollo 17*

INTRODUCTION

The exact origin of the name "Red Sea" already used by Herodotus in the 5th century BC is not known.

This great Greek historian often refers in his *Histories* to the "Erythraean" Sea, an adjective that means "red" in Greek. According to a legend, the origin of the name is supposed to be linked to a mythical king called *Erythros*.

More scientifically it is thought that the term alludes to the reddish color of the waters in particular conditions (which are actually quite rare) created by the exceptional proliferation of a minute unicellular alga, called *Trischodesmium erythraeum*.

In actual fact, it is more likely that the term "red" was used by Greek or Phoenician sailors to refer to the color of the coasts of this sea, consisting for the most part of rocks that were reddish due to their high content of iron oxides.

The ancient Egyptians, who already plowed these waters in the third millennium BC, called it by a completely different name "the great green sea". The first historical references to navigation on the Red Sea date from the time of Pharaoh Sahure (5th Dynasty) and of Pepy II (6th Dynasty) and it is known that at the time of the 12th Dynasty the Egyptians had a base for maritime trade in the vicinity of what is today the small town of Quseir.

The Red Sea coasts consist of rocks rich in iron ore that are therefore often reddish in color

The Greek historian Herodotus of Halicarnassus

Queen Hatshepsut (1479-1457 BC), the Egyptian Museum, Cairo

The Egyptians coasted the shores of the Red Sea to reach the distant Land of Punt, an area that has not yet been precisely located but that probably corresponded to the region of the Horn of Africa, where they acquired exotic animals, elephant tusks, valuable hardwoods, gold, spices and especially incense and myrrh, substances not to be found elsewhere and necessary both for religious rites in their temples and for embalming the dead.

The most famous expedition to Punt

An incense tree

Some specimens of Red Sea fauna depicted in the temple of Hatshepsut at Deir el Bahari (West Thebes)

took place during the reign of Queen Hatshepsut who sent a fleet of five ships to this land under the command of Nehesi. This expedition, the account of which is still perfectly legible in the bas-reliefs on the queen's temple at Deir el Bahari (West Thebes), was a great success and the ships brought sticks of incense, thirty incense trees (*Boswellia canteri*), about eight hundred kilos of gold, a large quantity of *electrum* rings (an alloy of gold and silver), animal skins and live animals including giraffes, a cheetah and some baboons.

 12

The crews of Egyptian ships loading the valuable incense trees

The Israelites crossing the Red Sea pursued by the pharaoh's soldiers in a painting in the Doura Europos synagogue (Syria)

Coin depicting King Ptolomy III (298-286 BC)

The name of the Red Sea is associated with the biblical account of when Moses led the Israelites through its divided waters, which immediately afterwards broke over the Egyptian army that was in hot pursuit. Numerous books have been written about this story and some scholars have denied that it is based on historical truth. What is certain is that the Bible is not referring to a crossing of the Red Sea, but of the *Yam Suf* "Sea of Reeds" later mistakenly translated as "Red Sea".

Apart from the fact that no Egyptian annals report the episode, which makes one think that the number of people involved was very small, today it is thought that the "Sea of Reeds" must be geographically located in the area of the Bitter Lakes, to the north of Suez, and that the biblical story alludes to an exceptional tidal phenomenon that probably occurred in the 13th century BC at the time of Pharaoh Ramesses II (1279-1213 BC).

Many centuries later, Herodotus recounts how Pharaoh Necho (672-664 BC) had a fleet of ships built on the Red Sea and ordered Phoenician sailors to sail down its coasts and circumnavigate the African continent (*Histories*, II, 158-159). However, it was only a few hundred years later, at the time of the Ptolemaic sovereigns, successors of Alexander the Great, that trading ships began to sail the Red Sea regularly and fifteen or so ports were established along its banks, between Suez and the Strait of Bab el-Mandeb in the South.

Goods from the Somalian coasts, the Indian Ocean and the Orient were unloaded at the ports of Berenice or *Myos Hormos* (in the vicinity of today's Quseir) and from here they were transported overland along the ancient Wadi Hammamat road to the Nile Valley.

After 30 BC, the Romans, who had made Egypt a province of their empire, exercised complete

Frieze depicting a Roman Warship (Vatican Museums)

An Arab sailing ship. The Arabs dominated the Red Sea and Indian Ocean trade routes for centuries

manual" known today. With the fall of the Western Roman Empire the Red Sea trade routes were plied less and less and, after the Arab conquest of Egypt in 630 AD, they were debarred from western ships for several centuries.

This did not mean, however, that trade through the Red Sea was interrupted; western traders stopped in the Mediterranean ports of Alexandria and Damietta, while Arab ships undertook to transport goods from the African territories, the Indian Ocean and the Far East to Suez.

In the 15th century, Red Sea trade became enriched by a new product, coffee, a plant of the family Rubiacee for which the French botanist Antoine de Jussieu, at the beginning of the 18th century, created the genus *Coffea*, from the Arabic name *qahwa* that became *kahve* in Turkish and then "coffee" in English. This was a plant that originally came from the Abyssinian plateaux in Ethiopia, and was already

control over the navigation of the Red Sea, which had in the meantime acquired considerable importance, one merely has to remember that over one hundred ships set sail for India from the port of *Myos Hormos* every year and that the naturalist Pliny the Elder, who lived in the 1st century AD, recounts that the Roman empire spent 100 million sesterces every year on merchandise from India.

It was probably during this period that the so-called *Periplus of the Erythraean Sea* was written, an anonymous work that supplied "nautical instructions" necessary for navigating the area and can be considered the first "navigation

Page 15
The world map of the Arab geographer Al-Idrisi (1100-1166) held by the Bodleian Library, Oxford

The coffee plant
(Coffea arabica)

A Turkish dignitary tasting a cup of coffee

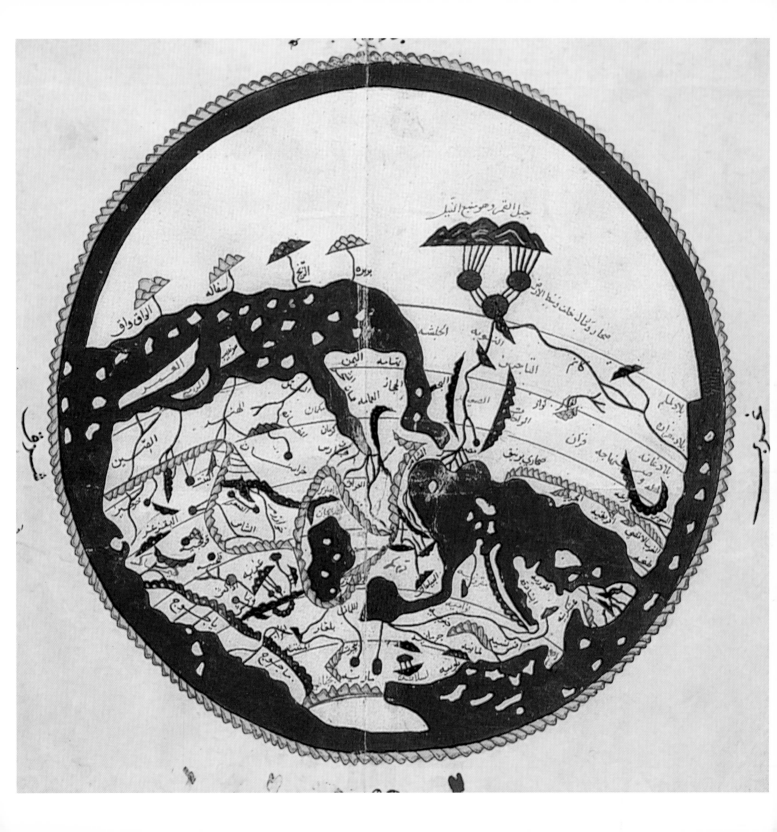

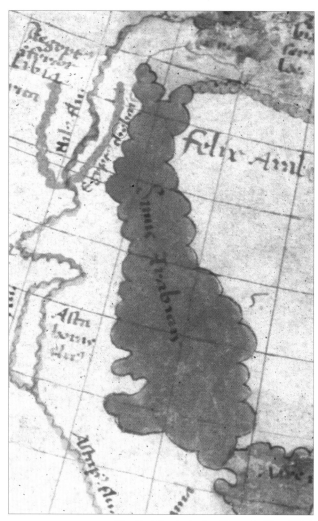

General view of the port of El-Tor in the 17th century

The Red Sea in Andrea Bianco's Atlas, 1436,
held by the Biblioteca Marciana, Venice

mentioned by the Muslim doctor Avicenna at the beginning of the 11th century.

Transplanted on the heights above the port of Mocha along the Yemenite coast of the Red Sea, it first spread throughout the Arab world and then to Europe, via the Venetian merchants who traded with the Turks, now the rulers of Constantinople. In the 16th century this picture changed greatly with the arrival of the Portuguese and with the discovery of new trade routes which, thanks to Vasco da Gama, opened up the so-called "way to the Indies" in 1498. Later, in 1512, Alfonso d'Albuquerque placed the Persian Gulf under Portuguese rule by occupying Hormuz, while in 1541, João de Castro set sail from Goa with around a hundred ships on a voyage of exploration up through the Red Sea to Suez, putting in at Quseir and El-Tor en route.

The Portuguese navigator
Vasco da Gama (1469-1524)

After the Spaniards took Lisbon in 1580, the power of the Portuguese, who for a century had held the trade monopoly with the Indies, went into decline. The English created the *East India Company* in 1600 and in 1664 the French established the *Compagnie des Indes Orientales*.

The great trade routes now no longer passed through the Red Sea since the transport of merchandise through the Suez isthmus to the Mediterranean was long, laborious and uneconomic and formerly flourishing ports like *Adulis* (Massaua), Quseir and El-Tor fell into decline.

The French conquest of Egypt in 1798 gave rise to

A portrait of Ferdinand de Lesseps (1805-1894) painted in 1853

research and projects for digging a canal to join the Red Sea and the Mediterranean, thus shortening the distance between Marseilles and Bombay by almost half, a good 5,400 miles. Despite thousands of difficulties and England's fierce opposition, thanks to the determination, enthusiasm and perseverance of the young French diplomat Ferdinand de Lesseps, work began on the canal in 1859 and it was completed ten years later in November 1869.

Thus a new era began for the Red Sea which became the focal point of the great modern trade routes.

The opening of the Suez Canal. The procession of ships bearing the guests on its way to Ismailia on 19 November 1869

CITIES UNDER THE SEA

The madrepores that form the coral reefs construct complex edifices that are organized like actual cities under the sea.

Table corals (Acropora sp.) on the island of Giftun (Hurghada)

THE CORAL REEF

The *coral reefs* are the result of the construction work carried out by billions of living organisms called **coral polyps**.
These formations, which first appeared in their present form around 200 million years ago, have experienced periods of enormous development or virtual disappearance due to changing climatic conditions on our planet. In fact, in order to develop and multiply coral polyps need specific climatic conditions the most important of these being temperature, which must be between 20 and 30 °C.
To be able to build a reef these organisms must also have a symbiotic relationship with particular unicellular algae known as *zooxanthellae* that need a good deal of sunlight to activate the process of photosynthesis, which

As well as madrepores the coral reefs also consist of numerous brightly-colored soft corals or Alcyonacea that host the reef fauna, represented here by numerous Anthias

permits the calcium found in seawater to be transformed into a rigid structure or theca that encases the polyp.

For this reason the zooxanthellae prefer clear, shallow waters. The corals in symbiosis with them are thus known

The large table corals (Acropora sp.) may be over 2 meters in diameter

THE WORLD OF THE REEF

Coral reefs constitute an ecosystem that is vital to ocean life, whose importance in the conservation of the biological balance of the Earth is comparable only to that of the great tropical forests.
Coral reefs extend over a total area estimated to be approximately 280,000 square kilometers between 30° N and 30° S of the equator, and host a fauna that comprises 4,000 of the 27,000 known species of fish and are an essential food source for at least 95 developing countries.

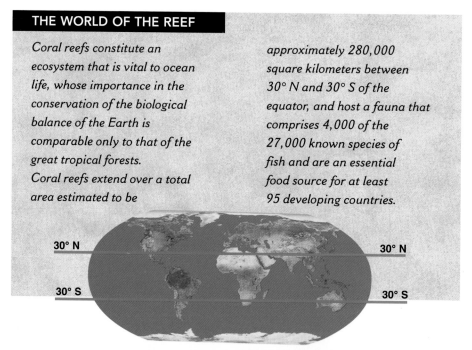

30° N   30° N

30° S   30° S

as "reef-building" corals or **madrepores**, while those without zooxanthellae are the so-called "soft corals" or **Alcyonacea**.

The particular climatic conditions that permit the growth of coral polyps are all to be found in the Red Sea, which therefore features highly developed coral reefs that cover an overall surface of 17,400 square kilometers, equivalent to 6.1% of the total estimated area of coral reefs in the world. In effect the Red Sea has clear, warm waters given that no rivers or industrial runoff flow into it since it is mostly surrounded by desert and it is also exposed to a great deal of sunlight. Its average salinity is therefore 41‰, far higher than that of all other seas.

The Red Sea came into being during the Tertiary Era, about 40 million years ago, when Asia began to separate from Africa, a process that is still going on at the incredible rate of 1.5 centimeters a year and is a basin a little over 2,000 kilometers long with an average width of around 300 kilometers. According to the geological time scale it is easy to calculate that, if the present speed remains constant, in 200 million years the Red Sea will be around 3,000 kilometers wide, almost the same as the Atlantic Ocean, and this is why it has been described as an "ocean in the making".

Because of the extraordinary diversity of its fauna the great variety of shapes and colors that make up its reefs, Captain Jacques Cousteau has described it as "the corridor of wonders" and long before him the Arabs called it the "garden of Allah". About 250 species of coral live in the Red Sea and the Gulf of Aqaba

THE RED SEA IN FIGURES

Length: *2,250 km*
Average width: *300 km*
Width at Bab el-Mandeb: *29 km*
Area: *438,000 sq.km*
Average depth: *2,000 m*
Maximum depth: *2,850 m*
Depth at Bab el-Mandeb: *134 m*
Average salinity: *41‰*
Maximum temperature: *30 °C*
Minimum temperature: *20 °C*
Average temperature: *25 °C*
Average hygrometry: *~70%*
   (in the morning)
Average hygrometry at Aqaba: *45%*
Species of fish: *1,248*
Species of endemic fish: *17%*
Species of coral: *~250*
Species of endemic coral: *8%*

alone has 218 species. The Red Sea reefs are basically well conserved and were not affected by the ocean warming in 1998 that led to the destruction of most of the reefs in the Maldives.

The area covered by coral reefs in the Egyptian part of the Red Sea is 3,800 square kilometers and between 60% and 80% of this consists of living madrepores. Today all these reefs are protected by the Egyptian government that since 1983 has created national parks to conserve an ecosystem that is unique in the world, still healthy but fragile and potentially at risk.

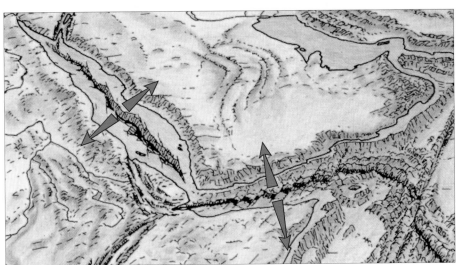

The separation of Asia from Africa led to the formation of the Red Sea

The polyps of a soft coral of the genus Tubastrea *extend their tentacles, especially at night, to capture food particles transported by the currents*

anemones and jellyfishes belong to the group (or *phylum*) of Cnidarians, from the Greek *knide* meaning "nettle". The symbiotic algae called *zooanthallae* are to be found in the endoderm that surrounds the gastric cavity. Coral polyps possess tentacles that become extended usually at night and permit them to capture floating food particles and direct them to their mouths. Cnidarians are carnivores and feed on plankton, tiny shrimps and detritus and comprise three main groups:

1. Anthozoa (from the Greek *anthos* = flower + *zòon* = animal) which, according to the number of tentacles, are divided into Octocorallia including Alcyonacea and gorgonians, and Hexacorallia that include madrepores, sea anemones and antipatars (like black coral);

2. Hydrozoa (from the Greek *hydros-* = aquatic + *zòon* = animal) including the fire corals (genus *Millepora*);

3. Skyphozoa (from the Greek *skyphos* = cup + *zòon* = animal) whose most well-known members are jellyfishes.

The structure of a coral polyp comprises an external theca or **ectoderm** lined on the inside by a thin layer of nervous fibers called **mesoglea** and an epithelium known as an **endoderm**.

The ectoderm consists of muscular epthelium cells that permit the contractions of the sensorial cells and of urticant cells called *cnidoblasts* containing an ampulla or *nematocyst* with a filament or *cnidocil* inside immersed in a stinging or paralyzing liquid that allows the polyp to capture its prey. For this reason all the madrepores and soft corals, sea

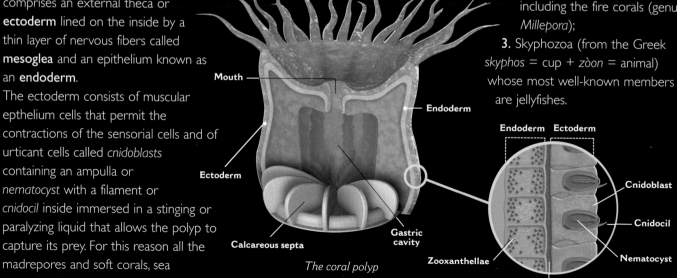

The coral polyp

QUEEN OF THE NIGHT

This splendid sea anemone looks like a small cone during the day but at night it turns into a flower that may be up to 40 cm tall and it spreads out its translucent tentacles.

Alicia mirabilis, *Hurghada*

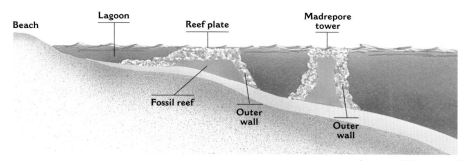

Beach | Lagoon | Reef plate | Madrepore tower | Fossil reef | Outer wall | Outer wall

Section of fringing reef

The zooxanthellae, the unicellular symbiotic algae that permit the calcium carbonate contained in the sea water to become fixed, are only present in Hexacorallia: it is estimated that in every cubic meter of madrepores there are approximately 30,000 zooxanthellae.

The madrepores, of which there are around 800 known species, are therefore responsible for the formation of coral reefs that are the largest constructions created by living organisms, whose importance for the Earth's survival is comparable only to that of the great tropical forests.

The madrepores construct coral reefs according to precise architectural rules that are influenced by various factors: depth, currents, the wave movement and light. From a morphological standpoint the reefs can be divided into three main kinds:

1. fringing reef
2. barrier reef
3. atolls.

In the Red Sea nearly all the reefs are fringing reefs.

The fringing reefs are formed close to the shoreline and grow toward the open sea.

They may have a lagoon that in

A typical fringing reef seen from the air

some cases extends even for about a hundred meters, and a stretch of madrepore towers that rise from the seabed to the surface for some twenty meters or so.

Fringing reefs gradually evolve into barrier reefs in which the lagoon may even be several miles in length.

The time it takes for coral reefs to form varies greatly depending on the madrepores that are present. Table coral like *Acropora* sp., for example, which is ramified can grow about thirty centimeters a year while *Porites* only increase by a few millimeters over the same period of time.

In the reef soft corals (Alcyonacea), hard corals (Madrepores) and Hydrozoa coexist in close contact with each other thus creating a complex ecosystem

THE TIRAN REEFS

The Strait of Tiran at the end of the Gulf of Aqaba has four impressive madrepore formations rising from the depths of the sea.

The Gordon Reef with the wreck of the Loullia *and the Thomas Reef*

Lobophyllia sp.

Favia sp.
Groved mosaic coral
Corallo mosaico
Mosaik-Koralle
Favia
Фавитес

Porites solida

Porites lutea

Galaxea fascicularis

Juncella sp.
Whip coral
Corallo a frusta
Peitschenkoralle
Gorgone fouet
Хлыстообразный коралл

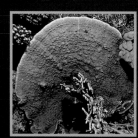

Turbinaria mesenterina
Salad coral
Corallo lattuga / Salatkoralle
Турбинария желтоволнистая

Paramuricea sp.
Red gorgonian
Gorgonia rossa
Rot-Gorgonie
Gorgone rouge
Красная горгония

Pachyseris speciosa

Favites sp.

Subergorgia hicksoni
Gorgonian sea-fan
Gorgonia a ventaglio / Hickson's Riesenfächer
Gorgone d'Hickson / Веерный коралл Хиксона

Millepora platyphylla
Fire coral / Corallo di fuoco
Feuerkoralle /
Уплощенная миллепора

Distichophora violacea

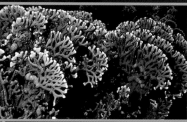

Millepora dichotoma
Fire coral / Corallo di fuoco
Feuerkoralle / Corail de feu ramifié
Разветвленная миллепора

Fungia sp.
Mushroom coral
Madrepora fungo
Pilzkoralle
Corail champignon
Грибовидный коралл

Plerogyra sinuosa
Grape coral / Madrepora uva
Blasenkoralle / Corail à bulles
Зеленый пузырчатый коралл

Acropora sp.

Acropora sp.

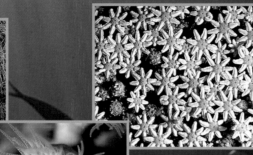

Antipathes sp.
Black coral
Corallo nero
Schwarze Koralle
Corail noir
Черный коралл

Tubastrea sp.

Tubipora musica
Organ-pipe coral
Corallo a canne d'organo
Orgelkoralle
Corail orgue
Красный органчик

Acabaria sp.

Stylophora pistillata

Pocillopora verrucosa
Raspberry coral
Madrepora lampone
Himbeer-Koralle
Corail framboise
Бородавчатая поциллопора

Sarcophyton sp.
Stalked alcyonarian
Corallo cuoio
Lederkoralle
Alcyonaire-champignon
Коралл саркофитон

Lithophyton arboreum
Broccoli soft coral
Corallo broccolo
Brokkoli-Koralle
Corail broccoli
Коралл-брокколи

Dendronephthya sp.

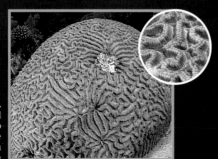

Platygyra sp.
Brain coral
Corallo cervello
Hirnkoralle
Corail-cerveau
Пластинчатая платигира

*A large colony of fire corals (*Millepora dichotoma*) arranged in a fan shape*

FIRE CORAL

Despite its name and its appearance, the so-called "fire coral" is not a coral but belongs to the Hydrozoa group that includes organisms that are extremely different in appearance and habits.

Fire corals have a calcareous skeleton like the madrepores, but a more complex structure. In fact, they comprise two kinds of polyp, one that ingests its prey and the other that has many cells containing a strong stinging substance.

For this reason the fire coral that belongs to the genus **Millepora,** when touched burns very painfully.

The larvae of the Hydrozoa are small jellyfishes that can move. Fire corals prefer very light, shallow areas (up to 15 meters deep) with currents.

Generally they are fan-shaped and grow perpendicular to the current, but if the current is very strong they take on the shape of a cone that opens toward the current.

The old houses in El-Tor are built of fossil madrepore

FOSSIL CORALS

The fossil coral reefs that are now to be found above the surface, as a result of the change in coastline that occurred at the end of the last ice age, contain many species of madrepore that are very similar to those of today.
The study of these fossil corals provides important data on environmental conditions 20,000 years ago.
In the photo: an example of fossil coral at Ras Mohammed (South Sinai).

Fossil coral reefs were used in the past as material for building the old Red Sea ports like El-Tor and Quseir.

In the historic center of El-Tor, administrative capital of South Sinai, you can still find many houses built

of blocks of fossil coral reef in which the different genera of madrepore such as *Porites*, *Goniastrea* and *Montipora* can be easily distinguished. Many stretches of the South Sinai coast, particularly the area around Ras Mohammed, consist of fossil coral reefs.

Some genera of madrepores such as Stylophora, Pocillopora *and* Acropora *grow a few centimeters below the surface and emerge from the water when the tide is very low*

THE WORLD OF GROTTOES

Often a few meters from the surface of the reef there are simple hollows or deep crevices that stretch into the fossil reef for dozens of meters thus becoming actual grottoes.
This is a very special world enveloped in shadow rather than darkness, in which the light sometimes penetrates through narrow fissures creating spectacular effects. These grottoes in the reef are home to a great variety of fauna including soft corals or Alcyonacea, sponges and many species of fishes some of which, like the Common bigeye (*Priacanthus hamrur*), the White-edged soldierfish (*Myripristis murdjan*) or the Lionfish (*Pterois miles*), are mostly nocturnal and take refuge in the grottoes during the daytime. Very often these fishes are red, since this color in water and in the absence of light, makes them completely invisible. Glassfishes (*Parapriacanthus* sp.) and Cave sweepers (Hatchetfishes) (*Pempheris vanicolensis*) with their bronze and silvery sheen that live in large schools that constantly disperse and reassemble at the passage of scuba divers.

A Saber squirrelfish
(*Sargocentron spiniferum)*

The world of the grottoes is inhabited by a great variety of multicolored fauna and is an infinite source of interest for scuba divers. Left, a White-edged soldierfish (Myripristis murdjan) and, center, a Diana's hogfish (Bodianus Diana)

*The Common bigeye (*Priacanthus hamrur*) is a nocturnal species often to be found in the grottoes*

*Cave sweepers (Hatchetfishes) (*Pempheris vanicolensis), *seen here in the photo, together with Glassfishes (*Parapriacanthus *sp.), are among the most common inhabitants of the grottoes*

Sometimes there are large openings in the ceilings of the underwater grottoes that ▶ create extraordinary light effects

*The wrecks are often home to many fauna. The photo shows a group of Onespot snappers (*Lutjanus monostigma*) among the remains of the wreck of the* Yolanda *at Ras Mohammed*

HOW MUCH IS THE REEF WORTH

If areas of reef are destroyed by ships or boats the Egyptian government has decided, apart from possible penalties in the case of proven guilt, to give fines according to the extent of the damage caused. These are calculated on the basis of 300 dollars for each square meter of reef destroyed for all the time needed for the growth of the new reef, which varies depending on the genera of madrepores from a few years for branching corals like the **Acropora** *to several decades for globular corals like the* **Porites.**

THE WRECKS

There are a large number of wrecks in the Red Sea due to the presence of numerous reefs just below the surface and the heavy daily sea traffic in the Gulf of Suez and the Gulf of Aqaba. In the past, especially in the years immediately after the opening of the Suez Canal (1869), many wrecks were caused by the inaccurate nautical maps of the time and the total absence of lighthouses and buoys to indicate potential dangers to navigation. Other wrecks, however, date from the time of World War II and resulted from attacks by the German airforce, like the famous *Thistlegorm* that sunk with all its cargo in the Gulf of Suez in 1941. In some cases the wrecked ships remained aground on the coral reef waiting to be broken up by the waves and corroded by the seawater as happened in the Strait of Tiran to the cargo ships *Loullia* (that was wrecked on Gordon Reef in 1981) and *Lara* (that ran aground on Jackson Reef in 1985). When the wrecks sink they are immediately colonized by madrepores and soft corals and turn into actual artificial reefs frequented by reef fish and large pelagic predators.

The wreck of the cargo ship Loullia *that ran aground on Gordon Reef in the Strait of Tiran in 1981*

AN ARTIFICIAL REEF

It only takes a few years to turn a wreck into an actual artificial reef. This ship, which sank in 1983, has already been colonized by Alcyonacea and madrepores and is home to a great variety of fauna.

The wreck of Ghiannis D. *in the Strait of Gubal*

FISHING

Fish is a very important source of food for the Bedouins and in general the populations that live along the Red Sea coasts. Even in the protected areas, where commercial fishing is strictly

The Red Sea Bedouins mostly fish with nets from the shore

Drying and salting are the only means the Bedouins have of preserving fish

banned, the Bedouins are allowed to fish for their own personal consumption and under the control of the authorities.

The Red Sea is so densely populated that you only have to throw a net into a few meters of water to catch a large quantity of reef fishes. The fishes that are not eaten immediately are dried in the sun and kept for those rare days

when weather conditions prevent fishing. Fishing is not a strictly male preserve, Bedouin women also catch octopuses and mollusks, like the Tridacna, which live in a few decimeters of water on the reef platform, with metal harpoons. Tuna fishes (in Arab *tuna*), goatfishes (*barbuni*), snappers (*bohar*) and emperorfishes (*shaur*) are the Bedouin fishermen's favorites.

Sometimes more well-off Bedouins use small boats for fishing

A Bedouin woman catching mollusks

GREAT WALLS OF FISH

Twospot snappers are often to be found in huge schools of thousands and they completely ignore scuba divers.

A school of Twospot snappers (Lutjanus bohar) at Ras Mohammed (Sinai)

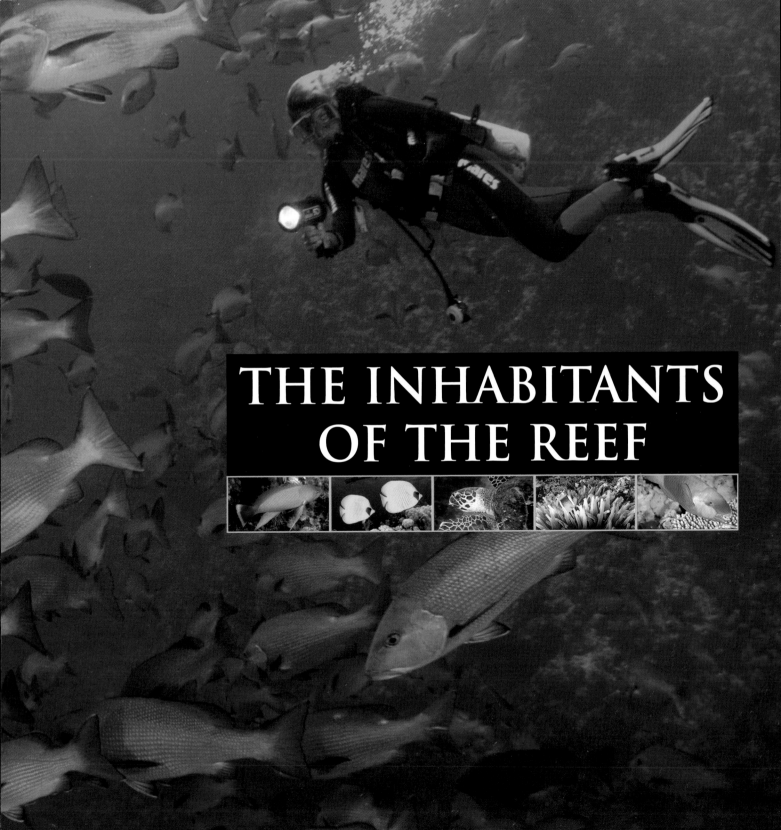

THE INHABITANTS
OF THE REEF

*A Salad coral (*Turbinaria mesenterina*) gives refuge to a vast population of Anthias*

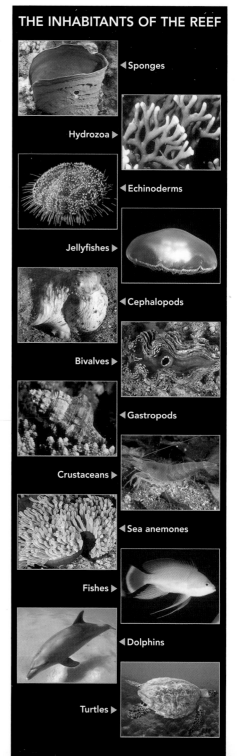

THE INHABITANTS OF THE REEF

◄ Sponges

Hydrozoa ►

◄ Echinoderms

Jellyfishes ►

◄ Cephalopods

Bivalves ►

◄ Gastropods

Crustaceans ►

◄ Sea anemones

Fishes ►

◄ Dolphins

Turtles ►

The coral reef is a complex ecosystem in which different kinds of living organisms coexist, each of which has its own precise function and has to find a way of surviving and reproducing.

The work of the reef-building corals (madrepores) is supported by the action of consolidating elements that produce or fix calcareous particles: Hydrozoa (fire coral), sponges, foraminifers and algae that are cementing agents. There are also other organisms like mollusks, echinoderms and soft corals that collect detritus that would otherwise be dispersed by the currents or that contribute toward building the coralline construction with their own calcareous skeletons. Numerous species of fishes live in the

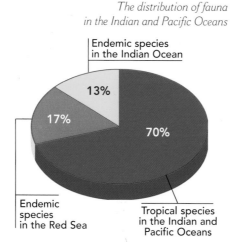

The distribution of fauna in the Indian and Pacific Oceans

Endemic species in the Indian Ocean

13%

17%

70%

Endemic species in the Red Sea

Tropical species in the Indian and Pacific Oceans

coral reef including butterflyfishes, parrotfishes, surgeonfishes and goatfishes, which are called **reef** species because they mainly feed on the inhabitants of the reef such as algae, coral polyps and small crustaceans. In the vicinity of the reef we find small and medium-sized predator fishes that are carnivores (**secondary consumers**) and feed on the above-mentioned fishes and, finally, large predators (**tertiary consumers**) like trevallies, barracudas and sharks, which feed on smaller predators.

Thus the so-called food pyramid is established at the bottom of which are the *phytoplankton* (**primary producers**) and the top consists of the tertiary

A school of trevallies patrolling their hunting ground in the vicinity of the coral reef

consumers. As we move upward to the top of the pyramid, the biomass diminishes and the size of the organisms increases: 10,000 kg of phytoplankton are needed to feed 1,000 kg of zooplankton, which in their turn feed 100 kg of mackerel that feed 10 kg of trevallies. Fishes occupy all the different levels of the food pyramid and thus acquire different functions that condition their structure, appearance and behavior. Parrotfishes and triggerfishes that feed on coral polyps have a very hard "beak" that permits them to break the madrepores; the fishes that feed on the seabed have particular structures known as *barbels*, which facilitate the task, while the large predators like the trevallies have slim bodies and powerful muscles that permit them to put on incredible bursts of speed to seize their prey.

In any event, competition for food in the reef is particularly fierce since all its inhabitants must eat to survive and reproduce.

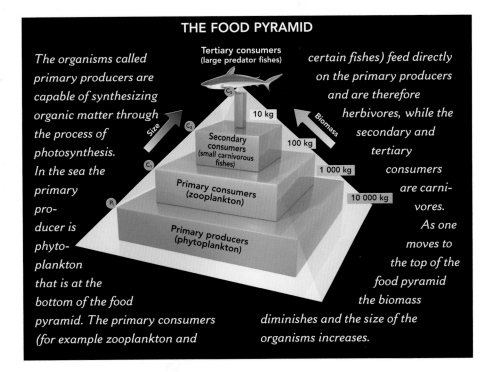

THE FOOD PYRAMID

Tertiary consumers (large predator fishes)

c_3

10 kg

Secondary consumers (small carnivorous fishes)

c_2

100 kg

Primary consumers (zooplankton)

c_1

1 000 kg

Primary producers (phytoplankton)

P_1

10 000 kg

Size

Biomass

The organisms called primary producers are capable of synthesizing organic matter through the process of photosynthesis. In the sea the primary producer is phytoplankton that is at the bottom of the food pyramid. The primary consumers (for example zooplankton and certain fishes) feed directly on the primary producers and are therefore herbivores, while the secondary and tertiary consumers are carnivores.

As one moves to the top of the food pyramid the biomass diminishes and the size of the organisms increases.

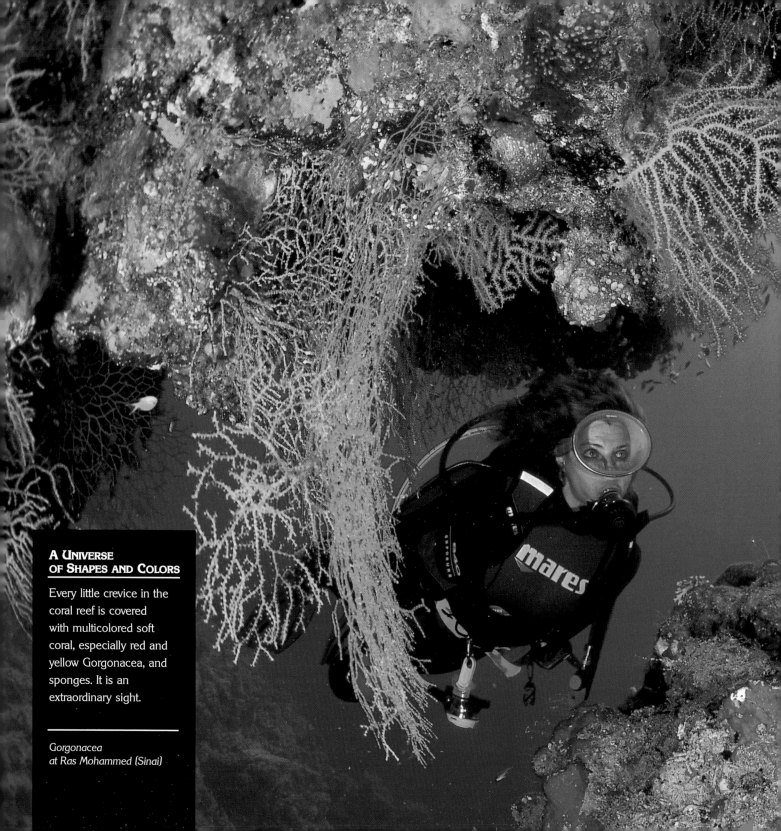

A UNIVERSE OF SHAPES AND COLORS

Every little crevice in the coral reef is covered with multicolored soft coral, especially red and yellow Gorgonacea, and sponges. It is an extraordinary sight.

Gorgonacea
at Ras Mohammed (Sinai)

SPONGES

Sponges are the most elementary of the pluricellular organisms, since they do not possess a nervous or digestive system, or circulatory apparatus. Sponges, of which there are over 5,000 species that differ considerably

Sponges very often host symbiotic algae or even small crustaceans

regarding shape and color, are filtering organisms that feed on plankton.

A sponge can filter a volume of water equal to that of its own body in about 20 seconds, and the larger varieties can process as many as 2,000 liters of water a day. Water enters the body of the sponge through a number of pores called *ostia* that are linked to a network of channels, and is expelled through an opening known as the *osculum*.

Many sponges have an internal skeleton composed of calcareous or siliceous elements, known as *spicules*, which are most important for classifying them.

In the most common sponges in the Red Sea (the class Demospongia) the spicules are composed of a protein similar to collagen, known as *spongina*. Some sponges may, at first glance, be

A calyx sponge

confused with coral. Sponges colonize large parts of a reef and exist at the most diverse depths, from just below the surface to 50 meters. There are over 25 species in the Red Sea.

Many fishes, such as angelfishes (family Pomacanthidae) and filefishes (family Monocanthidae), but also echinoderms and nudibranchs feed on sponges.

*An arborescent Fire sponge (*Latrunculia corticata*)*

*A delicate pink Siphon sponge (*Siphonochanalina siphonella*) and a black sponge (genus *Hemimicale*)*

S P O N G E S

BEAUTIFUL BUT DESTRUCTIVE

Sponges are essentially filtering organisms but this magnificent boring Red sponge (*Cliona vastifica*) is able to secrete strong acids that corrode and dissolve the madrepores.

Cliona vastifica *at Sharm el-Sheikh (Sinai)*

JELLYFISHES

Jellyfishes are mobile Cnidarians that belong to the class Scyphozoa, and are characterized by an umbrella shape and a gelatinous consistency. The Moon jellyfish (*Aurelia aurita*), one of the most common, usually frequents the open sea and lives on plankton, like the Upside-down jellyfish (*Cassiopea andromeda*) which instead prefers warm, shallow waters where it attaches itself to the sandy bottom in an upside-down position with its oral arms facing upward. The *Pelagia noctiluca*, with its typical mushroom shape, is so called because it becomes luminescent at night if stimulated by the wave movement, and feeds not only on plankton but also small fish. It is a pelagic species with a very nasty sting and is particularly dangerous, unlike the Upside-down jellyfish which causes only a slight itch if it touches the skin. Jellyfishes have separate sexes, and the larval forms (*planulae*) first become polyps that anchor themselves to the seabed and only later are transformed into jellyfish.

*The Upside-down jellyfish (*Cassiopea andromeda*) is usually to be found in lagoons with mangroves*

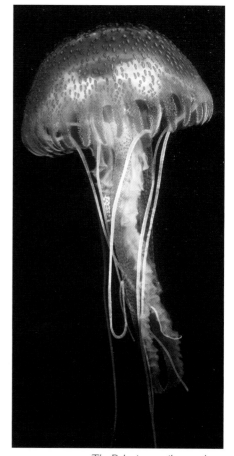

The Pelagia noctiluca, *whose sting causes painful burns, is a luminescent jellyfish*

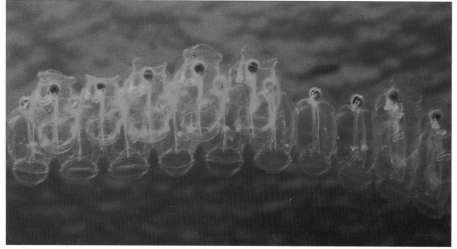

*Salps (*Thalia democratica*), which many scuba divers mistake for kinds of jellyfish, are highly evolved pelagic filtering organisms that belong to the phylum* Chordata *and to the family* Ascidiacea

*A Moon jellyfish (*Aurelia aurita*)*

JELLYFISHES

A COLORED UMBRELLA

Jellyfishes are mobile organisms composed of 95% water and, like all Cnidarians, have stinging cells called *nematocysts*.

A *Crown jellyfish*
(Netrostoma setouchina*)*

CRUSTACEANS

Crustaceans belong, together with insects and spiders, to the complex *phylum* Arthropoda, and are divided into two subclasses, the most important of which is that of the Malocostracans or Superior Crustaceans which includes shrimps, crabs, hermit crabs and lobsters. Malocostracans have a complex anatomy: they have a rigid, chitinous exoskeleton known as a *carapace*, a head with eyes, a thorax, an abdomen, and several pairs of claws (10 in the order of Decapods which is the principal one) that are used for walking, swimming and grasping. Morphologically speaking, Decapods can be divided into two groups: crabs, whose abdomen is smaller and tucked under the carapace, and shrimp and lobster, whose abdomen follows the shape of the carapace and is divided into various segments. The

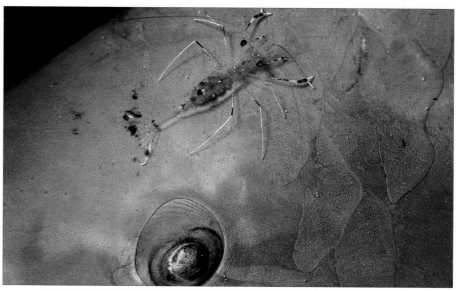

*A small Bruun's cleaning partner shrimp (*Urocaridella antonbruunii*) working on a Parrotfish (genus Scarus)*

structure of the hermit crabs, which have no exoskeleton, is a combination of the previous two groups. The latter can either swim or are obliged to walk on the seabed, according to their

characteristics. All Decapods are predators and capture their prey with their claws. There are over 260 species of Decapod Crustaceans in the Red Sea, 15% of which are endemic.

*This Blind shrimp (*Calliasmata pholidota*) is a species unique to the Red Sea and is only found at Ras Mohammed (Sinai) in a crack that opened on land in 1968, following an earth tremor*

CRUSTACEANS

THE CORAL CRAB

The Variable coral crab (*Carpilius convexus*) inhabits the crevices of the reefs, and the *Acropora* sp., and emerges at night to hunt its prey of mollusks and food particles.

Carpilius convexus *at Ras Mohammed, (Sinai)*

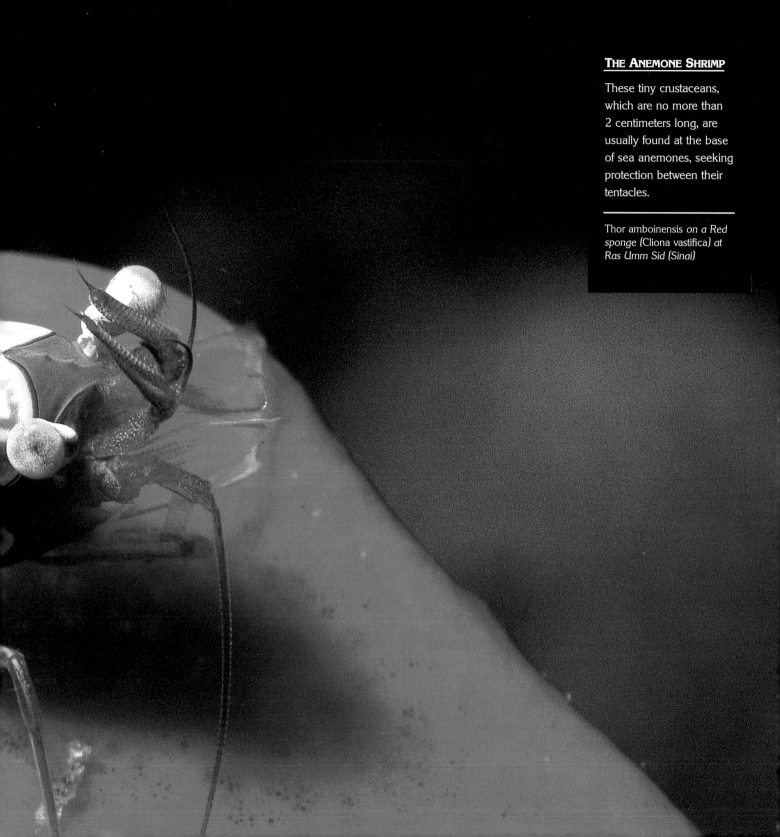

THE ANEMONE SHRIMP

These tiny crustaceans, which are no more than 2 centimeters long, are usually found at the base of sea anemones, seeking protection between their tentacles.

Thor amboinensis *on a Red sponge* (Cliona vastifica) *at Ras Umm Sid (Sinai)*

MOLLUSKS

Mollusks constitute a very complex and heterogeneous *phylum* (which includes over 80,000 species) and are characterized by a soft body in which a head with a mouth and eyes, a particular muscular structure known as a foot, gills, a siphon, and sometimes a shell, can be distinguished. Mollusks are divided into seven classes, three of which (Gastropods, Lamellibranchs and Cephalopods) are particularly important in the Red Sea. Gastropods generally have a single conical or spiral shell. According to the species, they can be carnivorous or herbivorous, but they all possess a foot that allows them

*A Triton (*Charonia tritonis*) on an* Acropora. *These Gastropods are the mortal enemies of the Crown-of-thorns starfish*

to move about. The Lamellibranchs or Bivalves are, instead, sedentary mollusks characterized by two valves (dorsal and ventral) with a hinge that allows them to open and close. The body is also distinguished by a mantle that covers

the internal organs, and a foot that allows them to attach themselves to a substratum (madrepores or rocks) or to bury themselves in the sand. The gills of the Lamellibranch species have assumed a filtering, as well as a breathing, function that permits them to feed on floating food particles. Finally, there is the third class composed of Cephalopods that are the most highly developed mollusks since they have tentacles instead of a single foot. They include cuttlefishes, squids and octopuses.

A POISON DART

The Conus textile *lives on the sandy bottom in shallow waters at a depth of between 1 and 5 meters. During the day it remains hidden in the sand, while at night it emerges to hunt small fishes that it kills by shooting venomous darts through its proboscis. Its toxin causes neuromuscular paralysis and can also be deadly to humans.*

The fearsome Conus textile *is a nocturnal predator with an elaborately patterned shell, but despite its beauty it can be deadly if not handled with care*

A GIANT MOLLUSK

The giant Tridacna is the
largest Lamellibranch that
inhabits the Red Sea, and
specimens weighing over
250 kilograms have been
found in the Indian and
Pacific Oceans.
The dazzling colors of
its mantle are created
by the zooxanthellae
present.

*A Tridacna (Tridacna gigas)
at Ras Nasrani (Sinai)*

NUDIBRANCHS

NUDIBRANCHS

Nudibranchs, commonly known as "sea slugs", are Gastropods without a shell. They are characterized by brilliant colors that ward off possible predators; in fact, the nudibranch's only protection is its high toxicity level that makes it inedible.

Nudibranchs are thus called because their gills are external and float in the water, taking the form of a small plume known as the *branchial plume* located on the dorsal side. On the ventral side there are two small antennae known as *rhinophores* that have an olfactory function.

There are more than 3,000 species of nudibranchs in the seas of the world and, although hermaphroditic, they reproduce by mating and fertilizing each other, and feed mainly on sponges and sea anemones.

Specimens of the genus Phyllidia, *characterized by large warts, are very poisonous*

A specimen of Four color chromodoris (Chromodoris quadricolor) *on a red sponge (genus* Latrunculia), *its favorite food*

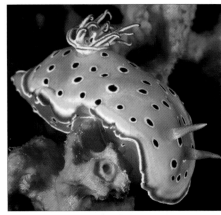

A Chromodoris kuniei *specimen with its typical mauve mantle*

*The eggs of the Spanish dancer (*Hexabranchus sanguineus*) are arranged in concentric wavy ribbons in the shape of a rose. Their toxicity discourages predators*

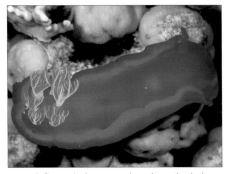

A Spanish dancer with its branchial plume visible, resting on a madrepore

DANCER OF THE NIGHT

At night the Spanish dancer's red mantle swirls very elegantly in the waters of the Red Sea. It is the most well-known nudibranch.

A *Spanish Dancer* (Hexabranchus sanguineus) *at Ras Mohammed (Sinai)*

OCTOPUSES, CUTTLEFISHES AND SQUIDS

Octopuses, cuttlefishes and squids, which belong to the Cephalopod class, are the most highly developed mollusks and their head, which has a very efficient ocular apparatus, is also the

A common octopus (genus Octopus)

most evolved. None of the Cephalopods have external shells except the Nautilidae (genus *Nautilus*), which are descended from mollusks that existed during the Late Cretaceous period, known as Ammonities, whose foot evolved into tentacles. The various species are distinguished according to the number of tentacles as follows:
- Decapods, which have 10 tentacles and an internal shell, like cuttlefishes and squids;
- Octopods, which have 8 tentacles and no internal shell, such as octopuses. All Cephalods have chromatographic cells and are able to change color according to their surroundings or "mood". Timid but very intelligent, Cephalopods are carnivorous and feed on fishes, mollusks and crustaceans.

*A Common cuttlefish (*Sepia prashadi*) hunting at night on the sandy bottom: Cephalopods move with the aid of a sophisticated reaction system, by expelling water through a siphon*

THE BIGFIN REEF SQUID

The Bigfin reef squid (*Sepioteuthis lessoniana*) is a large nocturnal predator and can measure almost 50 centimeters in length.

Bigfin reef squid (Sepioteuthis lessoniana) at Carless Reef

SEA URCHINS – CRINOIDS

SEA URCHINS AND CRINOIDS

Sea urchins, starfishes, and crinoids, although different in appearance, belong to the same group of marine organisms known as *echinoderms* (from Greek *echinos* = urchin + *derma* = skin) to which the holothurians (sea cucumbers) also belong. They are characterized by the absence of a head, their anatomic organization is based on pentaradial symmetry, and they have an unusual *aquiferous* system that by pumping water into the small tubefeet, known as *podia*, gives them a certain mobility. The skeleton of the echinoderm is composed of plates of calcite joined to each other, from which spines protrude, and the mouth with five teeth is located on the lower surface. Of particular interest is the Slate pencil sea urchin (*Heterocentrotus mammillatus*) with very

*Slate pencil sea urchin (*Herterocentrotus mammillatus*)*

strong spines, and the Diadem sea urchin (*Diadema setosum*) with long, very slender spines, both of which inhabit the reef plate. Far more dangerous is the Pin-cushion sea urchin (*Asthenosoma varium*), whose spines have venomous glands. Echinoderms feed at night on algae and small invertebrates. Crinoids, on the other hand, have a central body called a *calyx* and long arms with feathery pinnules arranged in the shape of a fan.

*The dreaded Pin-cushion sea urchin (*Asthenosoma varium*) with poisonous spines*

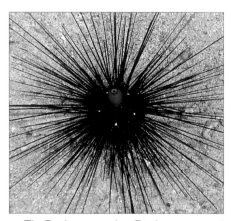

*The Diadem sea urchin (*Diadema setosum*) with its very delicate spines*

A FAN BY NIGHT

During the night this crinoid, firmly fixed to a madrepore, stretches out its feathered arms in a fan shape to capture the plankton carried by the current.

A brown Klunzinger's feather star (Lamprometra klunzingeri) at Ras Umm Sid (Sinai)

CROWN-OF-THORNS STARFISH

THE CROWN-OF-THORNS STARFISH

Starfishes are disk-shaped echinoderms with five arms, or *ambulacra*. They are usually harmless, but not always: the Crown-of-thorns starfish, or *Acanthaster planci* as it is scientifically known, is in fact a real scourge for

A scuba diver observes a Crown-of-thorns starfish, which is mainly a nocturnal creature

*A Crown-of-thorns starfish (*Acanthaster planci*) on an* Acropora *sp.*

coral reefs. It feeds on coral polyps, and when it becomes too prolific it is capable of destroying vast areas of reef. The Crown-of-thorns starfish literally invaded the seas of Australia in 1969 and the Red Sea in 1998, but the cause of this hyperproliferation is still a mystery, although it has been suggested that it can possibly be attributed to the decline in the number of gastropods known as Tritons (*Charonia tritonis*), their bitter enemy, in these waters.

The ambulacra of the Crown-of-thorns starfish secrete toxins that are lethal for madrepores and dangerous for humans and can give them a nasty sting

Rangers from the parks of Egypt have removed 144,000 Crown-of-thorns starfish from the Red Sea to save its reefs

A Fatal Encounter

Between 1998 and 2001, Crown-of-thorns starfish destroyed enormous areas of reef in Sinai and the Red Sea. This phenomenon, whose precise causes have not yet been determined, is now diminishing.

Acanthaster planci *on* Millepora dichotoma *and* M. platyphylla *at Gordon Reef, Strait of Tiran*

SEA TURTLES

TURTLES

Turtles are reptiles belonging to the Chelonian order, which have adapted to aquatic life and their sole link to the land is the fact that they lay their eggs in holes 50-70 centimeters deep, which they dig in sandy beaches about 5 meters from the water's edge. With respect to their land equivalent the tortoise, sea turtles have undergone various significant changes that have enabled them to adapt more easily to the habitat in which they live, such as forelimbs that have evolved into flippers; a smaller, lighter carapace (a sea turtle cannot retract its head and flippers) that enables them to float more easily and lessens resistance through the water (drag); a highly vascularized trachea that enables them to extract oxygen from the water, and lungs that exploit the oxygen to the full. There are 5 species of turtle in the Red Sea, but the two most important are the Green turtle (*Chelonia mydas*)

*The Green turtle (*Chelonia mydas*) is characterized by a rounded beak. Indiscriminate hunting has made it an endangered species*

*The sharply pointed beak typical of the Hawksbill turtle (*Eretmochelys imbricata*)*

and the Hawksbill turtle (*Eretmochelys imbricata*) which are also the only ones to reproduce in this area. They nest in the summer months on the beaches of the islands in the Red Sea, especially Giftun Saghir, Zabargad and Wadi Gimal. The Green turtle has a rounded beak and can grow to a considerable size (specimens have been found with a carapace 140 centimeters long, and weighing over 350 kilograms). The Hawksbill turtle, which is the more common species, is smaller (the

carapace is never longer than 90 centimeters), has a more pointed, hawk-like beak and overlapping carapace scutes, arranged rather like roof tiles. The Green turtle is the only herbivorous sea turtle and, unfortunately, its meat is a much-sought-after delicacy, while the Hawksbill turtle feeds on sponges and Alcyonacea, and its meat can be poisonous. Although they are both endangered species, the Green turtle risks extinction more than any other sea turtle on the planet.

A Friendly Encounter

A Hawksbill turtle
(*Eretmochelys imbricata*)
swimming near a coral
reef, looking for sponges
and Alcyonacea on
which it feeds.

Eretmochelys imbricata
near the Gordon Reef in the
Strait of Tiran (Sinai)

DOLPHINS

You often come across dolphins in the Red Sea, especially when sailing across the Strait of Tiran.
There are four genera of dolphins in the Red Sea, two of which, the *Tursiops* and *Stenella*, are the most common. Dolphins of the first genus are very large (they can reach a length of 2.5 meters), live alone or in small pods and in the Red Sea occur with the species *truncatus aduncus*, the Bottlenose dolphin,

The *Stenella longirostris*, also called the Spinner dolphin, is smaller with a more elongated snout, and lives in large pods that may number over 200.

Dolphins like to follow motorboats for fun, taking advantage of the fact that they are much faster: a dolphin can reach a speed of 50 kph without any effort.

More rare is the Grampus or Risso's dolphin (*Grampus griseus*) characterized by a paler skin that is often marked by scarring patterns, and by a large rounded head.

These dolphins are usually referred to as "beluga" by the local guides.

*A large Bottlenose dolphin (*Tursiops truncatus*)*

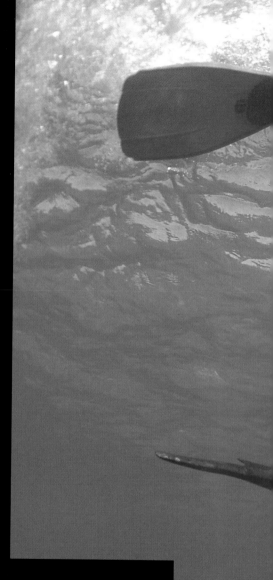

MAN'S FRIEND

A large Bottlenose dolphin (*Tursiops truncatus aduncus*) in the Red Sea plays with a bather. These dolphins are very sociable.

Bottlenose dolphin (Tursiops

THE DOLPHINS
AT SHAAB SAMADAI

The Spinner dolphins are
the most common in the
Red Sea.
A population of these
dolphins permanently
inhabits Shaab Samadai,
a reef ten or so miles
south of Marsa Alam.

---

*Pod of Spinner dolphins
(Stenella longirostris)
at Shaab Samadai*

DUGONGS

Dugongs, commonly known as sea-cows, are large mammals belonging to the order Sirenia that live in shallow sheltered bays, preferably fringed by mangroves, with sandy beds covered with thick carpets of seagrass, which are the only food of these timid, gentle giants that can be over two meters in length and weigh 300 kilograms. Their front flippers help them move and also direct the food to their mouth while their rudimentary back limbs are virtually hidden by their body mass. The upper lip is particularly developed and so prehensile it is a kind of small proboscis adapted to gathering food that consists wholly of seagrass (genus *Halophila*). The dugong community living in the Red Sea (*Dugong dugon*) comprises around 4,000 members and is the second largest in the world. Dugongs are becoming increasingly rare and are already an endangered species in the Red Sea. If they are to survive, everyone must help to protect them.

Seagrass (genus Halophila) *is dugongs' only food and they eat at least 50 kilograms per head a day*

*A large dugong (*Dugong dugon) *busy eating its usual ration of seagrass surrounded by young, Golden pilot jacks (*Gnathanodon speciosus) *that feed on tiny animals that live on the sandy seabed stirred up by the dugong during its huge meals*

DUGONGS

A TIMID GIANT

A large dugong swimming surrounded by its usual companions, young Golden pilot jacks (*Gnathanodon speciosus*)

___

A dugong (Dugong dugon) at Marsa Malek to the south of Quseir

RAYS

Rays belong to the class of the Chondrichthyes or cartilaginous fishes whose skeleton has no bony tissue that also includes sharks among the around 900 species, which is very much smaller than the class of the Osteichthyes or bony fishes that consists of over 28,000 species. Rays and sharks also have other features in common like the lack of a swimming bladder, the presence of

*This Panther torpedo ray (*Torpedo panthera*) is able to generate electric currents of between 40 and 200 volts to paralyze its prey and defend itself from predators. The electric organs are located laterally*

The stingray's tail has two spines connected to venomous glands

5 or 7 gill slits, and their teeth, which vary greatly in shape depending on the feeding habits of the different genera, are constantly replaced throughout their lifespan. Rays, with around 500 species, are subdivided into two large orders: the Myliobatiforma comprising stingrays,

manta and eagle rays and the Torpediniforma consisting of the torpedo rays. The Blue-spotted stingrays (*Taeniura lymma*) are the most common rays in the Red Sea, and though they have one or more venomous spines on their tails, they are timid and not aggressive.

*The Blue-spotted stingray (*Taeniura lymma*) lives on sandy bottoms and can be up to 70-80 centimeters long. Timid by nature these rays often hide in the sand, allowing only their eyes and spiracles to emerge. They feed on minute crustaceans, worms and small fishes.*

RAYS

A FREQUENT ENCOUNTER

The Blue-spotted
stingray prefers sheltered
bays and lagoons with
sandy bottoms. The two
large orifices located
behind the eyes
(*spiracles*) serve to pump
water into the gill slits,
since its mouth is
located ventrally.

*A Blue-spotted stingray
(*Taeniura lymma*) at
Ras Mohammed (Sinai)*

MANTAS — EAGLE RAYS

MANTA RAYS AND EAGLE RAYS

Manta rays and eagle rays are pelagic rays that do not live on the seabed but in the open sea and mostly feed on plankton.

In order to adapt to different needs, their pectoral fins have lengthened to become actual wings that they use to propel themselves along by flapping them rhythmically and "flying" through the water.

The Manta rays (*Manta birostris*) are the largest members of the Myliobatiforma and can weigh over two tons. Their head features two large cephalic fins used to direct the plankton on which they feed toward their mouth, and also to change direction when swimming.

*The Spotted eagle ray (*Aetobatus narinari*) is a very elegant swimmer and has a pointed snout and teeth strong enough to break the shells of the mollusks it feeds on*

Their tails lack venomous spines. You frequently come across manta rays especially during the summer months, in sheltered bays and where they seek food near the surface.

Often the large manta rays, which are solitary except during the breeding season, are accompanied by pilot fishes or, like the dugongs, by young Golden pilot jacks (*Gnathanodon speciosus*). Spotted eagle rays (*Aetobatus narinari*), thus named because their backs are speckled with small white spots, are much smaller than mantas and their wingspan is never more than 2.5 meters. Like stingrays and unlike manta rays, they have a long thin tail with venomous spines.

Though eagle rays spend most of their time in the open sea, they also frequent the sandy bottoms of bays and lagoons where they rest and hunt for food (small crustaceans, worms, mollusks).

They are often to be found in pairs or, more rarely, in small groups and the females that are ovoviparous give birth to between two and four pups once a year.

*Manta rays (*Manta birostris*) have very agile cephalic fins that they use to direct the plankton toward their mouth: 5 pairs of gill slits are located ventrally*

A GENTLE GIANT

The Manta ray is the
largest of all the rays
and its wingspan can
reach 7 meters.
It is often accompanied
by suckerfishes like
Remoras (*Echeneis
naucrates*) whose real
function is not known.

*A Manta ray (Manta birostris)
at Nama Bay (Sinai)*

LARGE BUT HARMLESS

Giant Manta rays have
a tail that lacks
venomous spines and
readily allow divers to
approach them.

*A Manta ray
(Manta birostris)
at Ras Mohammed (Sinai)*

SHARKS

Sharks are certainly the fishes that attract the most attention – for different and often conflicting reasons – from scuba divers, snorkelers and swimmers in general. Due to their alleged ferocity these creatures instil terror and have an evil reputation. No other fish has been the protagonist or subject of so many novels and feature films as the shark. In actual fact, things are very different from how they are usually shown on screen.

Every year a total of around no more than fifty attacks on people are recorded (and those are mostly in Australia and South Africa, there are none in the Red Sea), while tens of thousands of sharks are killed by man for their liver or fins, the ingredients of

*The Scalloped hammerhead shark (*Sphyrna lewini*) has a curiously-shaped flattened head, due to its large number of receptors (the* ampullae of Lorenzini*), which permit it to perceive with greater precision the electric fields emitted by its potential prey*

a soup that is a favorite delicacy in the Far East. Around forty species of shark have been identified in the Red Sea, but there are only about fifteen common ones including the small, timid Whitetip reef shark (*Triaenodon obesus*), the Gray reef shark (*Carcharhinus amblyrhynchos*), the Leopard shark (*Stegostoma fasciatum*), the Scalloped hammerhead shark (*Sphyrna lewini*) and the Tawny nurse shark (*Nebrius ferrugineus*).

Sharks are very different in shape, size and feeding habits, but have some

*The Gray reef shark (*Carcharhinus amblyrhynchos*) is quite common in the Red Sea: it can reach a length of 2.5 meters*

A POTENTIAL DANGER

The Gray reef shark feeds on fish and crustaceans and has an unpredictable nature. It is often found in schools, is active particularly at night, and can become aggressive if fed.

A Gray reef shark (Carcharhinus amblyrhynchus) at Ras Mohammed (Sinai)

SHARK WATCHING

Shark watching is
becoming an
increasingly widespread,
exciting underwater
activity that is not
dangerous, especially in
the central area of the
Red Sea. However, if the
sharks are fed, a
practice often adopted
by photographers, they
may become aggressive.

*Whitetip reef sharks
(Triaenodon obesus)
in the southern Red Sea*

SHARKS

points in common: they have no swimming bladder and to vary their weight they use another organ, the liver, that can be enormous (as much as a quarter of their total body mass) and contains an oil used for producing cosmetics.

Sharks swim by using their tail as a propeller and many species are forced to move about constantly in order to increase the circulation of water that enters through their mouth and comes out through their gill slits, thus making their respiratory system more efficient. Sharks have powerful muscles and are perfectly hydrodynamic.

They normally swim at an average speed of 5-10 kph, but when they decide to attack they can attain a velocity of 60-100 kph in a few

*The Leopard shark (*Stegostoma fasciatum*) though quite big is virtually harmless if not disturbed*

seconds. Their teeth vary in shape and size depending on their feeding habits; they are arranged in two parallel rows and are regularly replaced during the fish's lifespan.

Sharks have extremely good eyesight, a highly-developed sense of smell (they can pick up the presence of blood in the water when it is diluted as much as one part to four hundred million) and they have the capacity to perceive variations of one millionth of a volt per square centimeter in the electric fields emitted by potential prey, thanks to special receptor organs called *ampullae of Lorenzini*, after the Italian naturalist who discovered them in 1678.

The shark's fearsome teeth

Sharks are perfect biological machines at the top of the food pyramid and they play a major role in maintaining the ecological balance of the seas of our planet. Today these creatures are threatened by man and his activities: shark fishing has an estimated turnover of over 300 million dollars a year and it is calculated that 2.5 million sharks are killed for every man killed by a shark.

*The Tawny nurse shark (*Nebrius ferrugineus*) usually remains motionless on the bottom or in the crevices of the reef during the day and emerges at night to hunt its favorite prey: cephalopods, shrimps and sea urchins. It is placid and generally not a danger to scuba divers*

LORD OF THE SEA

The Whitetip reef shark
(*Triaenodon obesus*) is
the most common
shark in the Red Sea.
Timid and shy it can
often be seen in the
crevices and small
grottoes of the reef.

Triaenodon obesus
at Gordon Reef

THE LARGEST FISH

The Whale shark
(*Rhincodon typus*) is the
largest fish in the world. It
can be up to 18 meters
long and weigh over 40
tons, but it feeds only on
plankton and is harmless.
It is good-natured and
readily allows divers to
approach it.
It can be found in the
vicinity of the reef and
near the surface in
sheltered bays where
plankton is plentiful.

Rhinodon typus
at Sheikh Coast (Sinai)

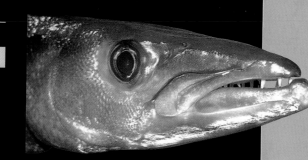

BARRACUDAS

Barracudas are extremely voracious predators that belong to the family Sphyraenidae, that live alone or in schools, and are widespread in all warm seas. They are tapering and hydrodynamic in shape, which allows them to put on extraordinary bursts of speed leaving their prey no chance of escape. Their silvery body has blackish stripes and is surmounted by a double dorsal fin; the head is pointed and the mouth contains a prodigious array of teeth. Barracudas are semi-pelagic, or rather, they live in the open sea but are often to be found in the vicinity of the reef, especially near walls that drop vertically into the blue, and they usually hunt during the day. The most impressive specimens belong to the species *Sphyraena Barracuda* or Great barracuda and can be up to 2 meters long. Adults are solitary and live near the surface, not far from the coral reef. Being curious by nature, they often approach divers not threateningly but

*The fearsome mouth of the Great barracuda (*Sphyraena barracuda*)*

to observe them at close quarters. Other smaller species like the Blackfin barracuda (*Sphyraena qenie*), which is the most common one in the Red Sea, live in large schools of hundreds or even thousands of individuals that often swim together in a vortex-like formation, which can be seen in the area of Ras Mohammed, especially in the summer months (July-August). There has been much discussion as to whether barracudas should be considered dangerous and some Great barracuda attacks on people have been reported in the literature. In actual fact, the barracudas' aggressiveness is linked to their voracity and it is usually only directed toward other fish.

*A small school of Blackfin barracudas (*Sphyraena qenie*)*

A VORTEX OF FISH

Very often during the
summer months, at
Shark Reef in
Ras Mohammed Park,
it is possible to see
thousands of
barracudas swimming
together in a vortex-like
formation, for reasons
that are still not known.

*A school of Blackfin
barracudas (Sphyrnae qenie)
at Ras Mohammed (Sinai)*

MORAYS

Despite their fierce appearance morays are rather timid creatures and attack divers only if really provoked. Their snake-like shape and considerable size (certain specimens of Giant moray can be over 2 meters long), their striking mouth, that is always kept half-open and armed with fearsome teeth, are certainly frightening.

If, however, you approach them with due caution you realize that they are not at all aggressive. However, it is best not to be too friendly and not

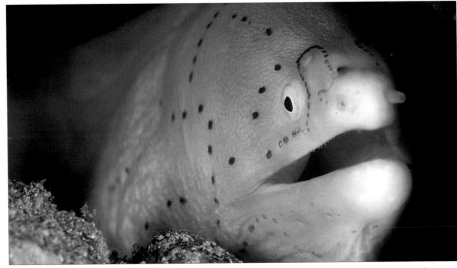

The small Gray moray (Sidera grisea) is very common and prefers the outer slopes of the reef in the vicinity of sandy bottoms. Often juveniles live in pairs or small groups

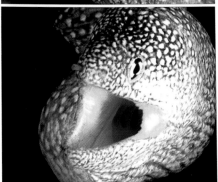

The Yellowmouth moray (Gymnothorax nudivomer)

touch or stroke them, or, even worse, feed them, a moray's bite is not only very painful but also causes dangerous infections.

Their skin is not covered with scales but with a mucous that permits them to slip easily into the narrow passages between the madrepores.

During the day they usually live partially hidden in the crevices of the reef with only their heads emerging to observe what is going on around them.

They leave their lair at dusk and hunt fishes and crustaceans, their favorite prey, at night, relying mostly on their very acute sense of smell, since they have two nostrils consisting of simple orifices in front of the eyes, and another two nostrils that form small protuberances on the snout.

Morays swim with a typical undulating movement since they do not have pectoral fins. Their teeth curve inward and give their prey no chance of escape and it is often devoured whole. A characteristic feature of morays is their two small, rounded branchial openings. Morays keep their mouth half open to increase the flow of water in their respiratory apparatus and thus improve blood oxygenation.

There are around fifteen species belonging to the family Muraenidae in the Red Sea. The morays most commonly found in the Red Sea are the Giant moray (*Gymnothorax javanicus*), the Yellowmouth moray (*Gymnothorax nudivomer*) that comes out of its lair even during the day, and the small Gray moray (*Siderea grisea*).

THE LARGEST MORAY

The Giant moray (*Gymnothorax javanicus*) is the most common moray in the Red Sea and also the largest; despite its threatening appearance it is not aggressive.

*Giant morays
(Gymnothorax javanicus)
at Ras Mohammed (Sinai)*

EELS

The general word "eel" refers to the members of different families (Heterocongridae, Congridae, Ophichthyidae, Plotosidae) that are all snake-like in shape.
Some species of the family Ophichthyidae look just like snakes and the Banded snake eel (*Myrichthys colubrinus*) even imitates the colors of the real sea snakes, which are extremely poisonous, to ward off possible predators.

The illusion is almost perfect, but if you observe these completely harmless eels carefully you will note that, unlike sea snakes, they have a pair of minute pectoral fins.

The most well-known species in the eel family is definitely the Garden eel (*Gorgasia sillneri*) that is very timid and ready to hide in its lair at the slightest sign of danger. It can be up to 40 centimeters in length and lives in colonies of hundreds that never move from their lairs, a long channel dug into the sand whose walls are cemented with a secretion emitted by a special gland on their tails.

*The Garden eel (*Gorgasia sillneri*)*

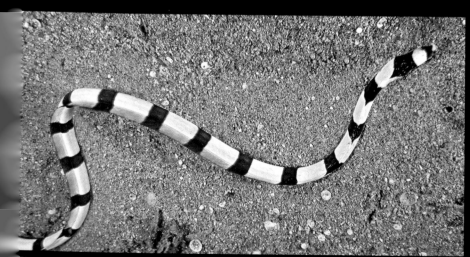

*The Banded snake eel (*Myrichthys colubrinus*) is completely harmless but its coloration imitates that of the poisonous sea snakes from which it is distinguished by its two minute pectoral fins.*

GARDEN EELS

On the sandy bottoms of some bays at a depth of between 10 and 25 meters it is quite easy to find colonies of Garden eels with a large part of their body emerging from the sand to catch the particles of plankton they feed on. It is pointless to try and approach them because at the slightest movement the eels withdraw into their lairs.

Gorgasia sillneri at Dahab (Sinai)

LIZARDFISHES AND FROGFISHES

Lizardfishes (genus *Synodus*), are so called because the shape of their head is similar to that of a lizard, and like land lizards they remain motionless for a long time on sandy bottoms in shallow waters partially hiding in the sand (Sand lizardfish or *Synodus dermatogenys*) or resting on their pelvic fins on a madrepore (Variegated lizardfish or *Synodus variegatus*), ready to attack their prey that consists of tiny crustaceans or fishes.

Despite their rather small size (they are never more than 30 centimeters in length), lizardfishes are voracious predators with a deep mouth and long pointed teeth.

*The Variegated lizardfish (*Synodus variegatus*) remains motionless for a long time on madrepores ready to attack its prey with great speed*

Frogfishes (genus *Antennarius*) are, by contrast, experts in camouflage and it is easy to be only a few centimeters from them and not be able to see them. They can turn different colors from yellow to red or white and stay in the very same place for weeks on end.

They feed mainly on small and medium-sized fishes and even lionfishes.

*The painted frogfish (*Antennarius pictus*)*

*A frogfish (genus *Antennarius*) perfectly camouflaged on a red sponge*

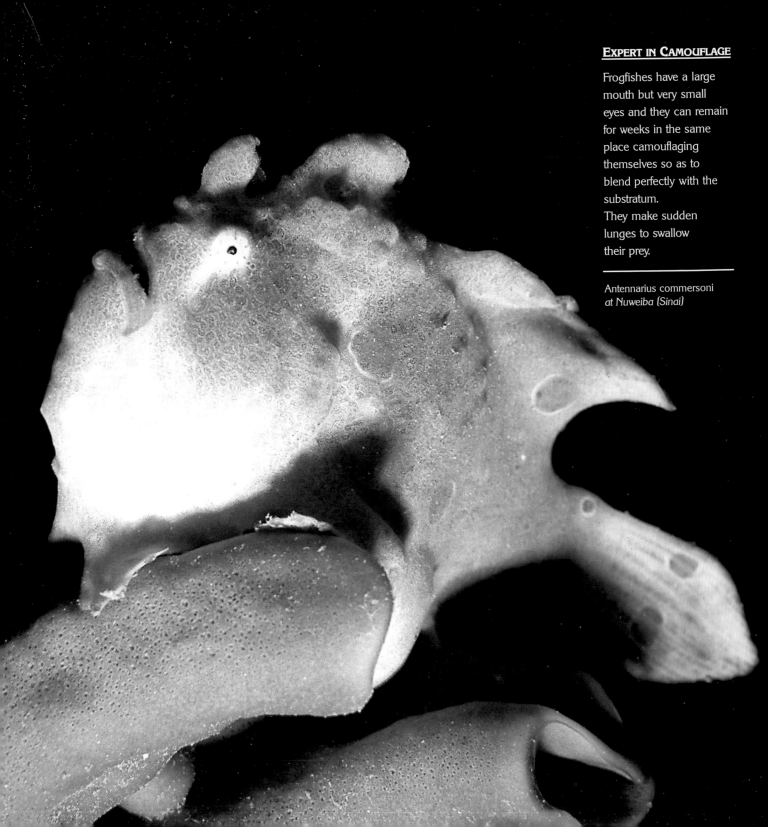

EXPERT IN CAMOUFLAGE

Frogfishes have a large
mouth but very small
eyes and they can remain
for weeks in the same
place camouflaging
themselves so as to
blend perfectly with the
substratum.
They make sudden
lunges to swallow
their prey.

Antennarius commersoni
at Nuweiba (Sinai)

CROCODILEFISHES

Unmistakable in appearance, motionless on sandy or detrital bottoms, the Flathead crocodilefish (*Papilloculiceps longiceps*) with its flat body and triangular head with huge mouth is immediately reminiscent of its fearsome reptilian counterpart. The Crocodilefish is, in fact, harmless and sedentary by nature and allows divers to approach it freely; only when it is really provoked does it move a few meters in search of peace.
It has a highly developed protruding lower jaw and its eyes are large, move rapidly and are very protuberant. If you examine them closely you can see that the pupil is covered by a special, irregular fringed eyelid.
The Crocodilefish is never more than

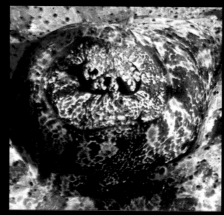

The crocodilefish's pupil is covered by a special fringed eyelid

70 centimeters long and likes waters that are not too deep (up to about 20 meters), where it lies in wait motionless and so well-camouflaged that its prey that consists of crustaceans and small fishes, swims right up close; it then pounces on it with astonishing speed and swallows it.

The Flathead crocodilefish (Papilloculiceps longiceps) has protuberant eyes and a large mouth

THE GUARDIAN OF THE WRECK

The Flathead crocodilefish (*Papilloculiceps longiceps*) also frequents wrecks. It is a solitary species, though it is sometimes found in pairs and can be up to 70 centimeters in length.

Papilloculiceps longiceps *on the deck of the* Thistlegorm *(Strait of Gubal)*

SEA HORSES - PIPEFISHES

SEAHORSES AND PIPEFISHES

Seahorses and Pipefishes are both characterized by an elongate body encased in a series of bony rings and belong to the numerous, and not yet completely known, family Syngathidae. These creatures, which are between 7 and 18 centimeters in length, are so well camouflaged they become virtually invisible and in the future the number of species (over 200, 31 of which live in the Red Sea) is destined to increase.

They have a long tube-like mouth with no teeth that acts like a powerful suction pump and is able to suck up the small crustaceans and invertebrates they feed on.

The most well-known members of the family Syngathidae are the seahorses of the genus *Hippocampus*,

The Thorny seahorse (Hippocampus histrix) has a body covered in spines

characterized by the angle of the head to the body that resembles that of a horse (in Greek *hippos* = horse). These fishes, which are rather rare in the Red Sea, swim in a vertical position, with the aid of their dorsal fins and they use their

prehensile tail to anchor themselves to algae or madrepores.

Pipefishes, represented by the genera *Corythoichthys*, *Doryrhamphus* and *Solenostomus*, swim horizontally in the grottoes and crevices of the reef.

The Many-banded pipefish (Doryhamphus multiannulatus) lives in the grottoes of the reef, often in pairs

THE SEAHORSE

These fishes live in shallow water and preferably among algae where they can find the tiny crustaceans they feed on more easily. The males carry the eggs for 4-5 weeks in a sort of pouch, where the female deposits them after they have performed a kind of mating dance in a vertical position with their tails entwined.

Hippocampus fuscus *among the algae (genus* Posidonia*) at Dahab (Sinai)*

LIONFISHES

Lionfishes (erroneously also called scorpionfishes since they belong to the family Scorpenidae) owe their name to the very long rays on their dorsal and pectoral fins that resemble a lion's mane.

Predators that are mostly nocturnal, during the day lionfishes (genus *Pterois*) live in the crevices of the reef, wrecks, sheltered areas and grottoes where they are often to be found covering the ceiling.

When they leave their daytime refuges at dusk, they swim slowly and very elegantly around the reef, unlike other Scorpenidae that lead virtually motionless lives, they are

*A Common lionfish (*Pterois miles*) on a boring sponge (genus* Cliona*)*

capable of sudden impressive bursts of speed to catch their prey of shrimps and especially small fishes such as glassfishes, which are their favorite.

Lionfishes live in pairs or groups and inhabit all parts of the Red Sea. Here you can find the Common lionfish (*Pterois miles*), the Tailbar lionfish (*Pterois radiata*), which is distinguished by its filiform rays, and the rarer Shortfin dwarf lionfish (*Dendrochirus brachypterus*).

Lionfishes are not frightened of divers and allow you to come quite close, though it is best to observe them with caution and not to touch them, if they feel threatened they may react by attacking the intruder.

Though they are not aggressive these fishes are quite dangerous, since their dorsal rays, connected to venomous glands, can give extremely painful, though not deadly stings.

*The Shortfin dwarf lionfish (*Dendrochirus brachypterus*), quite rare, is a species related to the Common lionfish*

BEAUTIFUL BUT DANGEROUS

The dorsal rays of the Common lionfish are plumed and covered with an interradial membrane. These fishes are sought after by photographers and aquarium enthusiasts, because they are so elegant.

Pterois miles
at Sharm el Sheikh (Sinai)

STONEFISHES

The Stonefish (*Synanceia verrucosa*) also belongs to the family Scorpenidae but, unlike lionfishes, it is a very bad swimmer and nearly always remains motionless on the seabed or on a madrepore. It can reach a maximum length of around 40 centimeters, is globular in shape and is an expert at camouflage, changing color to blend with its surroundings. Its skin has glands that secrete a viscous liquid that helps it adhere to sand and algae.

Its 12-14 dorsal spines are connected to venomous glands and its sting can be lethal if you happen to tread on it. The Stonefish's poison, similar to that of the lionfishes, is the strongest produced by all fishes and consists of thermolabile proteins including verrucotoxin (known as VTX) that seriously affect the circulatory and neuromuscular systems.

The Flathead scorpionfish (*Scorpaenopsis oxycephalus*) is also known as the "Fake stonefish", since it is often confused with the Stonefish. Both fishes are the same size, and have the same coloration and camouflage abilities, as well as the same habits, but their snouts differ in shape, that of the Flathead scorpionfish is more pointed and the lower jaw has many protuberances. Moreover, the Flathead scorpionfish has a downward-sloping mouth and its pectoral fins are more prominent.

*The Stonefish (*Synanceia verrucosa) is a very bad swimmer and moves very rarely*

Its ventral side is a bright orangey-red color, and is shown as a danger signal when it feels threatened, since its poison is similar to that of the Stonefish though less harmful.

The Flathead scorpionfish (Scorpaenopsis oxycephala) is often confused with the Stonefish

The eyes and mouth of the Stonefish are perfectly camouflaged

GROUPERS

There are over 300 species of groupers, which belong to the family Serranidae, and they are the predator fishes most typical of the coral reefs around which they live, feeding on cephalopods and crustaceans.

Most grouper species are between 40 and 90 centimeters long but Giant grouper (*Ephinephelus lanceolatus*) specimens reaching a length of 3 meters and weighing over 500 kilograms have also been recorded. The groupers in the Red Sea belong to the genera *Ephinephelus*, *Cephalopholis*, *Plectropomus*,

*The Malabar grouper (*Epinephelus malabaricus*) remains motionless on the seabed in sheltered areas*

Aethaloperca and *Variola* and are quite common among the reefs where they hunt mostly during the day or at dusk, usually lying in wait for their prey.

The largest groupers, like the Arabian grouper (*Epinephelus tauvina*) or the Potato cod (*Epinephelus tukula*), which can reach a length of 2 meters, often remain motionless on the sandy bottom or near wrecks which they sometimes inhabit.

Groupers are solitary fishes with territorial habits and are able to change color according to their age, their surroundings and even their "mood".

They can also change sex; in fact, groupers are born female and turn into males after becoming adults and laying their eggs in the open sea. Smaller groupers like the Coral grouper (*Cephalopholis miniata*) or the Moon grouper (*Variola louti*) are a primary food source, and are fished by the Bedouins of the Red Sea, who call them *koshar* in Arabic.

*The Moon grouper (*Variola louti*)*

VORACIOUS PREDATOR

The Coral grouper is one
of the most common
groupers in the Red Sea.
It frequents the seaward
slopes of the reefs and
areas with strong currents.

Cephalopholis miniata
at Jackson Reef (Sinai)

PLACID GIANT

The Potato cod
(*Epinephelus tukula*),
characterized by its sandy
coloration with dark
markings, can reach a
length of 2 meters, and
has sedentary habits.

Epinephelus tukula
at Rocky Island

ANTHIAS

Although much smaller and very different in appearance, the Anthias are closely related to the large groupers, since they also belong to the family Serranidae, characterized by the presence of a single rather long dorsal fin and tiny scales.

Though there are only four species of Anthias in the Red Sea they are the most common and typical fishes of the coral reef which they inhabit in very large schools.

The females differ from the males in that they are orange and do not have the long spine corresponding to the third ray of the dorsal fin.

Like all groupers, Anthias can change sex during their life cycle.

Male Anthias
(Pseudanthias squamipinnis)

The schools consist mainly of females, which outnumber the males 8 to 1. When a male dies, one of the females, usually the leader, changes sex in a week or two, assuming male attributes. Anthias are also predators but, given their small size, feed mostly on zooplankton.

Female Anthias (Pseudanthias squamipinnis)

ANTHIAS

GLINTS IN THE BLUE

Large schools of orange
Anthias, numbering
thousands, float near the
surface of the water close
to the madrepores and
the Alcyonacea, waiting
for the current to carry
the zooplankton on which
they feed toward them.
The orientation of the
Anthias enables scuba
divers to immediately
determine the direction of
the current.

Pseudantias squamipinnis *at
Tiran (Sinai)*

BREAMS AND GRUNTS

Breams belong to the family Sparidae and typically have a silvery body with two blackish bands in the region of the head, from which they get the name given to them by the locals: *abu kohol*, father of *kohol*, the black mineral cosmetic used by Bedouin women to accentuate their eyes.

The Doublebar bream (*Acanthopagrus bifasciatus*), which reaches a length of 50 centimeters, is either solitary or part of a large school, sometimes along with snappers (Lutjanidae) and spangled emperors (Lethrinidae).

The Doublebar bream lives in the shallows and in sheltered bays; it feeds on small crustaceans and mollusks, whose shells it cracks easily with its well-developed teeth.

Grunts, also known as sweetlips, belong instead to the family Haemulidae. They are called "grunts" because they sometimes emit grunting sounds produced by their laryngeal teeth; and "sweetlips" because they have particularly thick lips, probably to protect them from injuries that might be caused by the echinoderms or other invertebrates that they eat. The most well-known species of the family, which in the Red Sea includes the genera *Plectorhinchus* and *Diagramma*, is the Blackspotted grunt (*Plectorhinchus gaterinus*), which has a silvery body covered with black dots, and lives in pairs or in large schools, sometimes mixing with butterflyfishes. During the day, it stays beneath the table Acropora or shelters near the reefs, and goes out at night to hunt for food.

*The Doublebar bream (*Acanthopagrus bifasciatus*) has two distinctive black bands on its head*

GOLD AND SILVER

Blackspotted grunts (*Plectorhinchus gaterinus*) live in pairs or in large schools; the silvery coloration with black dots is typical of adults, while juveniles have three dark horizontal bands.

Plectorhinchus gaterinus at Dahab (Sinai)

SNAPPERS

Snappers (family Lutjanidae) are predators with a powerful body and single dorsal fin, a pointed snout with a wide protractile mouth and well-developed teeth.

According to the species, they are solitary or live in large schools, which sometimes include other genera such as butterflyfishes, in the immediate vicinity of the reef (less often in the open sea), and are usually to be found in the same areas, for example, Shark Reef at Ras Mohammed.

Snappers move constantly, never resting on the seabed, and hunt their prey of small fishes, such as fusiliers, and invertebrates, both during the day and at night. These fishes are very important commercially since their meat is highly prized and, together with emperors and groupers, they are much sought after by the local fishermen who refer to them generically as *bohar*.

The Twinspot snapper (*Lutjanus bohar*) is the most common species of the family and is so called because juveniles have two pale spots on the caudal fin; adults can reach a length of 90 centimeters.

The Onespot snapper (*Lutjanus monostigma*) is similar but smaller than the former, with a lighter coloration; it is active mostly at night and inhabits wrecks, grottoes and the sheltered areas of coral reefs.

*The Onespot snapper (*Lutjanus monostigma*) is mainly a nocturnal predator that inhabits sheltered places like grottoes, wrecks, and beneath the table Acropora.*

AN EXTRAORDINARY WALL OF FISH

Thousands of Twinspot snappers (*Lutjanus bohar*) gather at Ras Mohammed in the summer months, forming enormous schools.

Lutjanus bohar *at Ras Mohammed (Sinai)*

EMPERORFISHES

Two genera of emperorfishes, *Lethrinus* and *Monotaxis*, which belong to the family Lethrinidae, are to be found in the Red Sea.

They have silvery bodies and a single dorsal fin like the snappers, but a more pointed snout, thicker lips, two large incisors, and the position of their eyes make them different. Emperorfishes are nocturnal predators that hunt small fishes and invertebrates, but keep close to the reefs during the day.

The Spangled emperor (*Lethrinus nebulosus*) is the largest species of the family and can be as much as 80 centimeters long; it inhabits the sandy bottoms and algae beds where it hunts crabs and

*A small school of Spangled emperors (*Lethrinus nebulosus*)*

mollusks, its favorite food.

The Spangled emperor, referred to by the Arabs as *shaur*, and the Sky emperor (*Lethrinus mahsena*), a related species, are fished by the locals.

The Bigeye emperor (*Monotaxis grandoculis*) is the second most important genus of Lethrinidae in the Red Sea and gets its name from its large eyeballs.

It is either solitary or part of a small school, and keeps close to the reef.

*The Spangled emperor (*Lethrinus nebulosos*) is the most common species of the family*

*The Sky emperor (*Lethrinus mahsena*) has distinctive olive green bands*

BIGEYE EMPEROR

The Bigeye emperor
(*Monotaxis grandoculis*)
floats in the mid-waters,
often in small schools,
during the day.
At night it hunts its prey
that consists of tiny
invertebrates.

Monotaxis grandoculis,
Hurghada

FUSILIERS

Fusiliers and Sergeantfishes are among the most typical inhabitants of coral reefs. Forming schools of thousands, which sometimes include other species, fusiliers (which belong to the genus *Caesio*, from the Latin *caesius* = grayish-blue) patrol the reef front while searching for zooplankton, but are also to be found in the open sea.

Fusiliers reach an average length of 20-25 centimeters, have a silvery body with a bluish sheen, and a small protractile mouth. They also have a single dorsal fin and a forked, black-tipped caudal fin.

Living in schools is a means of survival for these fishes, whose remarkable speed and ability to change direction quickly enables them to escape from the barracudas, snappers and trevallies that feast on them.

They are active during the day, while at night they take refuge in the reef crevices and turn a reddish color to reduce their visibility.

The two most common species of fusiliers are the Suez fusilier (*Caesio suevica*) and the Lunar fusilier (*Caesio lunaris*), whose appearance and habits are similar.

The Suez fusilier is less bluish and has a gold band running around the base of the dorsal fin all the way down to the caudal fin and two white bands next to the black tips of the tail.

The Bedouins use fusiliers, which they call *haida*, as live bait for catching large predators.

*A Suez fusilier (*Caesio suevica*)*

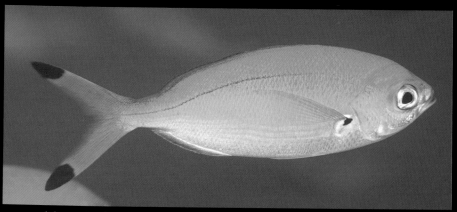

*A Lunar fusilier (*Caesio lunaris*) has a distinctive silvery coloration with a blue sheen*

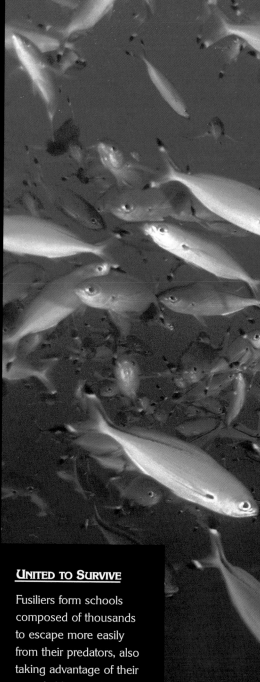

UNITED TO SURVIVE

Fusiliers form schools composed of thousands to escape more easily from their predators, also taking advantage of their remarkable speed.

Caesio suevica,
Ras Mohammed (Sinai)

GLASSFISHES

GLASSFISHES

Glassfishes form schools numbering hundreds or even thousands, moving constantly through grottoes, reef crevices, rifts that sometimes appear in madrepore towers, and wrecks. They are small fishes with a semitransparent body through which their internal organs can be glimpsed, covered with tiny silvery scales with a bronze sheen, which sparkle when caught in the sunlight or the flashes from the photographers' cameras, for

*A school of Red Sea dwarf sweepers (*Parapriacanthus ransonneti*)*

*The Hatchetfish, also called the Cave sweeper (*Pempheris vanicolensis*)*

whom they are a favorite subject. When scuba divers or predators pass by, the dense schools of glassfishes separate as if by magic, closing ranks again as soon as the threat has disappeared. For these fishes that have no means of defence, living in schools is a necessity since it prevents the predator from homing in on individual fish. In fact, there is often a solitary Redmouth grouper (*Aethaloperca rogaa*) swimming among the glassfishes, which seems to have a taste for them and, every so often, swallows one in a trice, as do the lionfishes. Glassfishes belong to the family Pempheridae that is composed of the genera *Parapriacanthus* and *Pempheris*. The Glassfish or Red Sea dwarf sweeper (*Parapriacanthus ransonneti*), which in the Red Sea reaches a maximum length of 10 centimeters, has a more transparent, tapering body, while the Cave sweeper or Hatchetfish (*Pempheris vanicolensis*), so called because its shape is reminiscent of a hatchet blade, is larger (it can reach a length of 18 centimeters), less transparent, more golden, and forms much smaller schools. These are both fishes with nocturnal habits: after dusk they leave their diurnal refuges and swim around the reef or in the open sea in search of plankton, their favorite food. The biological aspects of the Pempherids, which also have bioluminescent organs, have not all been clearly defined.

SPARKLING SPLINTERS

Thousands of glassfishes move constantly in the semidarkness of the grottoes. Their highly developed eyes can adapt to life in environments that are virtually dark.

Parapriacanthus ransonetti at Umm Gamar (Hurghada)

BATFISHES

These fishes have a distinctive laterally compressed, disk-shaped body, live in pairs or schools and, being very inquisitive, allow scuba divers to approach without any qualms, sometimes even following them. Batfishes belong to the family Ephippidae and two related and similar species are to be found in the Red Sea: the Circular batfish (*Platax orbicularis*) and the Longfin batfish (*Platax teira*), which has longer dorsal and ventral fins and a dark marking at the base of the anal fin. They are often seen near the external slope of the reef, in large grottoes or near wrecks. Their coloration is silvery with two dark horizontal bands, one across the eyes and the other, the operculum. The body can reach a diameter of over 50 centimeters.

Juveniles have a darker body and fairly tall dorsal and anal fins that are long in relation to the diameter of their body.

They prefer the sheltered shallow waters of the mangrove lagoons where, being a dark color, they blend with the dead leaves. Batfishes have diurnal habits and are omnivorous, even though they feed mainly on algae, zooplankton and small invertebrates.

*A school of Circular batfishes (*Platax orbicularis*) accompanied by a Hawksbill sea turtle (*Eretmochelys imbricata*)*

CLOSE ENCOUNTERS

A large school of Circular batfishes swirls around the seaward slope of the reef, fearlessly allowing scuba divers to approach and watching them with a certain interest.

Platax orbicularis
at Ras Mohammed (Sinai)

GOATFISHES

Goatfishes live in schools near the seabed that they search constantly for food. Their prey, usually small invertebrates that hide under the sand or in the madrepores, are dug out with two special protuberances called *barbels*, which are located beneath their mouth and are retracted in a kind of jugular sheath while they swim. Goatfishes belong to the family Mullidae and fifteen or so species inhabit the Red Sea.

The Yellowsaddle goatfish (*Parupeneus cyclostomus*), which can reach a length of 50 centimeters, has a golden yellow body that makes it easily identifiable; it frequents, in pairs or schools, areas exposed to the current and rich in madrepores into

*Some Yellowsaddle goatfish (*Parupeneus cyclostomus*) with their barbels retracted*

whose small crevices it inserts its long, highly developed barbels to extract minuscule fish on which, unlike the other members of the family, it feeds. The Yellowfin goatfish (*Mulloidichthys vanicolensis*) lives solely in large schools and has a distinctive silvery coloration with a horizontal yellow stripe running from the eye to the caudal fin.

*A pair of Yellowsaddle goatfish (*Parupeneus cyclostomus*) searching for food among the Alcyonacea*

GOATFISHES
IN FORMATION

An enormous school of
Yellowfin goatfish
swimming in close
formation. These fish
prefer sandy bottoms and
sheltered bays with no
currents, where they hunt
small invertebrates at
night, often together with
Bluestrip snappers
(*Lutjanus kasmira*). They
breed during the summer
months in the Red Sea.

Mulloidichthys vanicolensis
at Ras Mohammed (Sinai)

ANGELFISHES

Angelfishes (family *Pomacanthidae*) are the most colorful fishes that inhabit the coral reef, and together with butterfly-fishes (family *Chaetodontidae*) to which they are related, are the ones that brighten up their habitats the most. These fishes were only separated into two families in 1978, when the main characteristic that differentiates the Pomacanthidae (which comes from the Greek *poma* = cover + *acantha* = spine) from the Chaetodontidae, namely the long spine at the base of the operculum, was recognized. The Pomacanthidae have a laterally compressed, disk-shaped body of average size (between 15 and 50 centimeters long), tend to be solitary or, less often, live in pairs, and feed on zooplankton, algae and small invertebrates. They are protogynous

*The Royal angelfish (*Pygoplites diacanthus*) is one of the most colorful fishes of the coral reef*

hermaphrodites; in other words, the females change sex, as well as coloration, when they become adult. The Royal angelfish (*Pygoplites diacanthus*) has an orange body with eight light blue vertical bands edged in black; it inhabits sheltered areas, preferably near grottoes, and feeds on

algae, invertebrates and sponges. The Emperor angelfish (*Pomacanthus imperator*) is blue with yellow diagonal stripes while the Arabian angelfish (*Pomacanthus maculosus*), the largest member of the family (it can reach a length of 50 centimeters), is territorial and prefers sheltered areas without currents, where it lives at a depth of not more than 12 meters.

*An adult Emperor angelfish (*Pomacanthus imperator*)*

*A juvenile Emperor angelfish (*Pomacanthus imperator*) with its distinctive blue body and pale concentric ring markings*

THE BLUE ANGEL

The Arabian angelfish (*Pomacanthus maculosus*) has a blue body with a large golden yellow patch similar to Sinai or Africa in shape.

Pomacanthus maculosus,
Ras Mohammed (Sinai)

BUTTERFLYFISHES

Butterflyfishes are the most typical and well-known inhabitants of the reefs in the Red Sea. They belong to the family Chaetodontidae (from Greek, *kaite* = hair + *odontes* = teeth) which is composed of about 120 species (seven of which are endemic to the Red Sea) subdivided into 10 genera.

These fishes are flat and disk-shaped with a rounded caudal fin, and their coloration is distinguished by bright hues in which yellow predominates, apparently acting as a warning to other fish to keep out of their territory. Butterflyfishes are generally territorial, remaining within an area that can be as large as 1,200 square meters; they are rarely solitary, living more often in pairs or large schools. These fishes have a small protractile mouth and are active during the day while at night they prefer to withdraw into the crevices of the madrepores. They feed mainly on coral polyps but also small larvae, Hydrozoa, polychaetous worms, zooplankton, and sometimes algae.

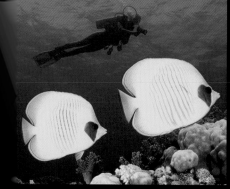

*The Masked butterflyfish (*Chaetodon semilarvatus*) is a species endemic to the Red Sea*

*A school of Red Sea bannerfish (*Heniochus intermedius*): a ray of the dorsal fin is extended like a flag and their coloration is distinguished by light and dark diagonal bands*

EATING TO SURVIVE

A large school of Striped butterflyfishes searching for food among the crevices of a large madrepore (genus *Porites*). This is also a species typical of the Red Sea.

*Striped butterflyfishes (*Chaetodon fasciatus*) at Ras Nasrani (Sinai)*

HAWKFISHES

Hawkfishes are small nocturnal predators (no more than 22 centimeters long) that belong to the family Cirrhitidae, thus called because its members have tiny tufts of filaments, *cirrhi* in Latin, at the end of their dorsal fin rays. The structure of the pectoral fins allows these fishes to

The cirrhi at the ends of the hawkfish's dorsal rays

attach themselves to and climb madrepores, fire corals and gorgonians, and position themselves at strategic points from which they can survey everything around them, just like the birds after which they are named. Once they have secured a good position, hawkfishes remain motionless, sometimes for hours, waiting for the tiny fishes, crustaceans and zooplankton on which they feed to come within range. As soon as they get close, the hawkfish pounces on them with lightning speed and swallows them. The two most common species of Cirrhitidae in the Red Sea (species that are difficult to observe, however) are the Longnose hawkfish (*Oxycirrhites typus*) which perches mostly on gorgonians, and Forster's hawkfish (*Paracirrhites forsteri*).

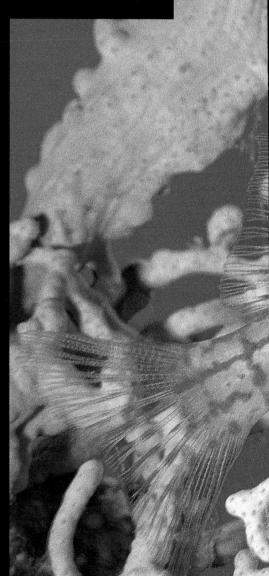

*A Forster's hawkfish (*Paracirrhites forsteri*) waiting patiently on a fire coral (genus* Millepora*) for shrimps or tiny fishes to swim past*

ANEMONEFISHES

ANEMONEFISHES

The anemonefish is probably the most well-known fish in the world thanks to the recent Disney film *Finding Nemo* in which it stars. Anemonefishes, together with sergeantfishes, pullers or chromises and damselfishes, belong to the huge family Pomacentridae which, composed of over 320 species – 35 of which inhabit the Red Sea – is the one most frequently found at coral reefs the world over.

The Red Sea anemonefish (*Amphiprion bicinctus*) has a yellowish-orange body, which is darker dorsally and has two whitish bands edged in black. This species is endemic to the Red Sea and lives, usually in pairs, in close association with sea anemones such as the Magnificent anemone (*Heteractis magnifica*), Bulb tentacle anemone (*Entacmaea quadricolor*) and Long tentacle carpet anemone (*Stichodactyla gigantea*), in which it makes its home. This is a perfect example of commensal symbiosis: the anemonefish cannot live without the sea anemone that hosts it and to which it is most faithful, while the anemone can survive alone,

*A Red Sea anemonefish (*Amphiprion bicinctus*) in front of a Magnificent anemone (*Heteractis magnifica*)*

although it benefits from the presence of its symbiont.

The anemone has urticating tentacles, to which the anemonefish is immune thanks to special glands that produce a protective substance, and it provides a refuge that keeps predators at bay. In its turn, the anemonefish protects the anemone from other fishes that like to eat its tentacles, such as butterflyfishes (genus *Chaetodon*). In fact, anemonefishes are extremely aggressive and do not hesitate to attack anything that gets dangerously close to their host.

*Large sea anemones like this Magnificent anemone (*Heteractis magnifica*), can host more than one pair of Red Sea anemonefishes (*Amphiprion bicinctus*)*

COMMENSAL SYMBIOSIS

The Red Sea anemonefish is protected by the tentacles of its sea anemone which defends it from predators like butterflyfishes.

Amphiprion bicinctus on a Bulb tentacle anemone (Entacmaea quadricolor), Naama Bay (Sinai)

CHROMISES, DAMSELFISHES, SERGEANTFISHES

Like the anemonefishes, sergeantfishes (genus *Abudefduf*), pullers or chromises (genus *Chromis*) and damselfishes (genus *Dascyllus*) are members of the family Pomacentridae. Sergeantfishes are represented by two fairly related species, the Sergeant major (*Abudefduf vaigiensis*) and Scissortail sergeant (*Abudefduf sexfasciatus*) which differs from the first in that the lobes of its caudal fin have black edges. These fishes

*The Sergeant major (*Abudefduf vaigiensis*)*

and fusiliers are the most common of the reef, where they live in large schools, feeding on plankton, algae and small invertebrates.

There are three Chromis species, two of which can be found throughout the Red Sea: the Bluegreen puller (*Chromis viridis*) and the Half-and-half chromis (*Chromis dimidiata*).

Both are often associated with the Banded dascyllus (*Dascyllus aruanus*) and live in schools between the branches of the madrepores (genera *Acropora* and *Pocillopora*), among which they hide at the first sign of danger. Damselfish is the name given to the species of the genera *Amblyglyphidodon*, *Dascyllus* and *Pomacentrus*, all of which are characterized by their small size (from 6 to 14 centimeters in length), a terminally positioned mouth (at the point where the dorsal and ventral sides meet) and an elongate body.

The Domino
(*Dascyllus trimaculatus*)

The Whitebelly damselfish (*Amblyglyphidodon leucogaster*) and the Yellowflank damselfish (*Amblyglyphidodon flavilatus*) live in schools and feed on algae, zooplankton and small invertebrates. The Sulphur damselfish (*Pomacentrus sulfureus*), a solitary fish living beneath the Acropora branches, exists on a similar diet, as does the Domino (*Dascyllus trimaculatus*), and is characterized by a white spot on either side of its dark gray body – and a third in a frontal position in the case of juveniles – and often lives with anemonefishes in the sea anemones.

Bluegreen pullers (Chromis viridis) *live in large schools among the madrepore branches* (genera Acropora *and* Pocillopora)*, hiding at the first sign of danger*

The Sulphur damselfish (Pomacentrus sulfureus) *has a distinctive golden yellow body*

SILVERY DAMSEL

A Whitebelly damselfish (*Amblyglyphidodon leucogaster*) in front of a gorgonian. This species with a silvery body is fairly widespread and lives on zooplankton and algae.

Amblyglyphidodon leucogaster,
Sharm el-Sheikh (Sinai)

NAPOLEONFISHES

The Napoleonfish (*Cheilinus undulatus*) gets its name from its large frontal hump that resembles the French Emperor Napoleon's hat.

It is the second largest fish of the reef, after the Giant grouper (*Epinephelus lanceolatus*): scientific literature records a specimen measuring 229 centimeters in length and weighing 191 kilograms, but Albert Falco, the legendary captain of the *Calypso* (Captain Cousteau's research ship), recounts that during his famous dive to the wreck of the *Thistlegorm* on 17 March 1955, he encountered a Napoleonfish that he estimated was 3 meters long.

The Napoleonfish belongs to the family Labridae, which is distinguished

*A small Cleaner wrasse (*Labroides dimidiatus*) at work*

by the enormous variety of its members (over 500 species). In fact, the small Cleaner wrasse (*Labroides dimidiatus*), which eliminates parasites and food particles from the bodies of other fishes in special areas of the reef, known as "cleaning stations", belongs to the same family. Like all Labrids, the Napoleonfish uses only its pectoral fins to swim and is active during the day; it is solitary, although it sometimes pairs off, lives at a depth of between 1 and 60 meters, and is mainly sedentary. It feeds mostly on invertebrates, including prickly sea urchins, and some poisonous species like boxfishes, but does not refuse other types of food; for example, in the past many divers (especially photographers, although it was forbidden) used to offer the Napoleonfish hardboiled eggs, which it loved. Unfortunately, these harmless, gentle giants are becoming increasingly rare and the species is endangered by overfishing.

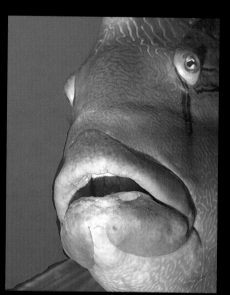

The Napoleonfish's fleshy lips allow it to eat prickly sea urchins

TIMID BUT INQUISITIVE

The Napoleonfish (*Cheilinus undulatus*) has a timid nature, but being inquisitive it lets scuba divers, who in the past had the bad habit of feeding it, get very close.

Cheilinus undulates at Sharm el-Sheikh (Sinai)

PARROTFISHES

Parrotfishes get their name from their two powerful incisor teeth which create a "beak" like that of a parrot, and the fact that they have the same flamboyant coloring as their namesake. Their strong teeth enable them to crush madrepores while searching for food, which mostly consists of algae.

Parrotfishes belong to the family Scaridae and are related to the labrids, some of whose characteristics they share, such as their particular way of swimming, and there are about 80 species all told.

In the past this number was overestimated, since the members of one single species can have markedly different colorations, according to whether the fishes are males, females or juveniles, and this makes classification very difficult.

During the night parrotfishes take refuge in the reef crevices, wrapping themselves in a mucus membrane, probably to ward off predators

In fact parrotfishes, like labrids, are protogynous hermaphrodites and change sex from female to male, and hence also the color of their body, during their lifespan.

*A male Red Sea steep-headed parrotfish (*Chlorurus gibbus*)*

The powerful "beak" of a parrotfish can break the hard madrepores

CREATORS OF BEACHES

Parrotfishes crush madrepores with their "beak", expelling them in the form of fine-grained sand: each fish is able to produce hundreds of kilos of sand a year and thus the species is responsible for the formation of many coralline beaches.

A female Red Sea steep-headed Parrotfish (Chlorurus gibbus) at Ras Umm Sid (Sinai)

SURGEONFISHES AND UNICORNFISHES

Surgeonfishes, represented by the genera *Acanthurus* and *Zebrasoma*, get their name from the pair of blades as sharp as scalpels – located on each side of the caudal peduncle, and retractile where some species are concerned – which can inflict deep wounds on contact.

These fishes belong to the family Acanthuridae whose characteristic features are an oval body, single dorsal fin, and small mouth in a terminal position. All members of this family are mainly diurnal, and herbivorous, mostly eating algae. Due to the strong sunlight algae proliferate on the reef platform where

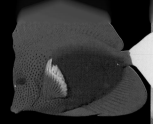

Blue sailfin tang
(Zebrasoma xanthurum)

you often see surgeonfishes, alone or in pairs, at a depth of only a few dozen centimeters, although they sometimes go deeper.

Unicornfishes also belong to the family Acanthuridae (genus *Naso*) and are so called because at the adult stage many species possess a prominent frontal "horn" like that of their mythical counterpart. Unicornfishes which have one or two pairs of non-retractile blades, are more gregarious than surgeonfishes, and some species feed on zooplankton rather than algae.

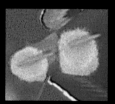

The unicornfish's sharp "scalpels"

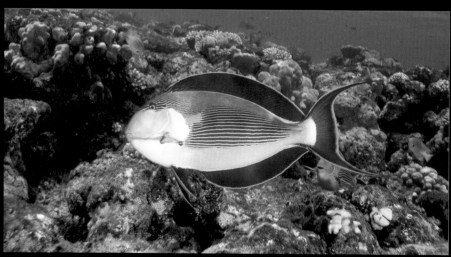

The Sohal surgeonfish (Acanthurus sohal) *is the most common of the surgeonfishes and is often seen near the reef platform where it can easily find the algae on which it feeds*

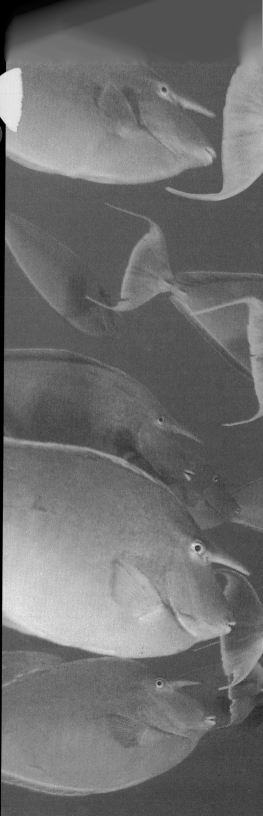

A WALL OF UNICORNFISHES

Thousands of Blue spine unicornfishes, which prefer areas with strong currents, gather at Ras Mohammed in the summer months. They have two pairs of blades at the base of their tail, which, unlike those of surgeonfishes, are non-retractile.

Naso unicornis,
Ras Mohammed (Sinai)

TREVALLIES

Trevallies, belonging to the family Carangidae, are voracious predators whose body structure allows them to put on extraordinary bursts of speed, giving their prey no hope of escape; in fact, speed is the preferred weapon of this fish which can travel as fast as 50 kph.

The Goldbody or Orange-spotted trevally (Carangoides bajad) *is able to swiftly change color*

In the Red Sea, the members of this family, which is also well-represented in the Mediterranean, are subdivided into 47 species. They have a sturdy, laterally compressed, silvery body, characterized by a rather narrow caudal peduncle and a powerful, strongly forked tail.

They live in the open sea where they breed, by laying floating eggs, and make swift forays to the seaward slope of the coral reefs in areas where there are strong currents.

They tend to be more active in the early morning and at dusk, and feed mostly on reef fishes, never refusing glassfishes, Anthias and crustaceans. The most daunting member of the family Carangidae is the Giant trevally (*Caranx ignobilis*): this fish can reach a length of 175 centimeters, and weigh over 60 kilograms.

*The Bluefin trevally (*Caranx melampygus*) is easily identified by the color of its fins, and hunts in small schools near the seaward slope of the reef, in grottoes and in wrecks*

GANGS OF PREDATORS

The Bigeye jackfish, one
of the most common
trevallies, is often to be
found at Ras Mohammed
in the summer months,
where it gathers in large
schools, sometimes
forming circles, and
carries out rapid forays
to the reef.

Caranx sexfasciatus
at Ras Mohammed (Sinai)

TRIGGERFISHES

If you think sharks are the most aggressive fish in the Red Sea you have not met a Giant triggerfish (*Balistoides viridescens*) during the breeding season which, in the Red Sea, takes place during the summer months (July–September) when these animals dig holes in the sandy bottom to lay their eggs, they stir up so much sand that it remains suspended in the water and is visible from afar. At this time, the unwary scuba diver who gets too close is immediately attacked and sometimes pursued for long distances.

Triggerfishes (family Balistidae) can reach a considerable length (as much as 75 centimeters) and are characterized by a sturdy, laterally compressed body with two dorsal fins,

*The small Arabian picassofish (*Rhinecanthus assasi*) lives alone or in pairs on the sandy bottom, feeding on crustaceans and worms. It is never more than 30 centimeters long and is harmless*

a large head and a relatively small terminal mouth with four strong teeth. The anterior dorsal fin is composed of three erectile spines connected by a membrane, which the fish uses to anchor itself firmly to the crevices in the reef, and whose mechanism is similar to that of the ancient ballista. Triggerfishes swim in a very unusual way, using only the posterior dorsal and the anal fin, and can also propel themselves backwards.

Like parrotfishes, they can crush the madrepores, but unlike the former they are carnivorous and feed mainly on invertebrates (mollusks, crustaceans, worms and even sea urchins).

*The Blue triggerfish (*Pseudobalistes fuscus*) is both solitary and territorial, lives on the sandy bottom and becomes aggressive during the breeding season in the summer*

*The Orange-striped triggerfish (*Balistapus undulates*) is not very aggressive and feeds on algae and invertebrates*

TRIGGERFISHES

A DANGEROUS ENCOUNTER

The Giant triggerfish is
the most aggressive and
dangerous fish in the
Red Sea, and can
reach a length of
75 centimeters.
It is extremely territorial
and does not hesitate to
attack scuba divers
who get to close to its
nest, inflicting very
dangerous bites.

Balistoides viridescens
at Tiran (Sinai)

PUFFERFISHES AND PORCUPINEFISHES

Pufferfishes belong to the family Tetraodontidae, which derives from the Greek *tetra* = four + *odontes* = teeth, since they possess four fused teeth. This particular formation permits them to easily crush the shells of the mollusks and crustaceans on which they feed.

They do not have ventral fins and propel themselves slowly with their pectoral fins and anal fin, and are also able to swim backwards.

In the face of danger they can "puff" up, filling their extensible gastric sac, which can actually double in volume, with sea water.

This is also a characteristic of porcupinefishes which belong to the closely-related family Diontidae, whose members have a body covered with strong spines. All Tetraodontids are extremely dangerous if eaten: their innards contain a strong poison called *tetrodotoxin* that can be lethal.

A Yellow-spotted burrfish (Cyclichthys spilostylus) puffed up to ward off a potential enemy

The Star pufferfish (Arothron stellatus) can reach a length of more than one meter, and inhabits sandy bottoms and sheltered bays. It lives on invertebrates, sponges and coral polyps

The Yellow-spotted burrfish (Cyclichthys spilostylus) is covered with spines

A HOST
OF SUITORS

During the mating
season, Masked pufferfish
(*Arothron diadematus*)
gather in large schools
composed mainly of
males who court a far
smaller number of
females.

Arothron diadematus
at Ras Mohammed (Sinai)

A WORLD TO BE PROTECTED

Today, the coral reefs of our planet, the largest structures created by living organisms in the world, are endangered. The causes are various, some being natural, others linked to the presence and activities of man, but the effects are devastating: coral polyps are dying and, consequently, madrepores are turning a typically whitish color (a phenomenon known as "bleaching"), and what were once paradises filled with life are becoming real underwater deserts.

The main natural causes are linked to ocean warming and to the strong influence of periodical warm currents, such as the notorious *Niño*, which destroyed vast areas of madrepore in the Indian Ocean in 1979 and especially in 1998, and affected 90% of the reef surfaces in certain areas. Other natural causes are the hyperproliferation of the

Crown-of-thorns starfish (*Acanthaster planci*) which has damaged enormous sections of the Great Barrier Reef in Australia, reefs in the Pacific Ocean and, to a lesser extent, those in the Red Sea. Man is also responsible for causing considerable damage to the coral reefs through population increase and the various types of degradation arising

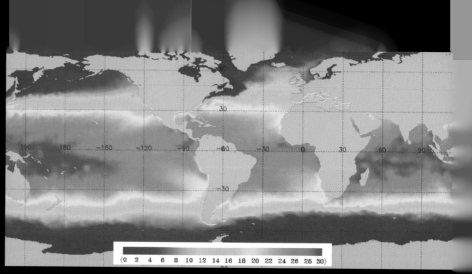

Ocean warming threatens the coral reef's survival

Reefs in the Red Sea are still in a good state of conservation

*The Crown-of-thorns starfish (*Acanthaster planci*) has destroyed vast areas of reef*

Dead madrepores turn a typical whitish color (phenomenon of bleaching)

from this. Overfishing reef species: it is estimated that over 40,000 tons of reef fishes, consisting mainly of groupers and Napoleonfishes are imported to the Far East every year, and that Hong Kong alone imports more than 6,400 tons of shark fins, meaning that over 28 million sharks have been killed; rampant tourist and industrial development in sensitive areas; and the large number of scuba divers and boats that converge on immersion sites, are just some of the main threats to the fragile world of the coral reef. In Sinai, for example, the

Overfishing changes the natural balance of the coral reefs

The excessive number of boats and scuba divers at immersion sites damages the reefs

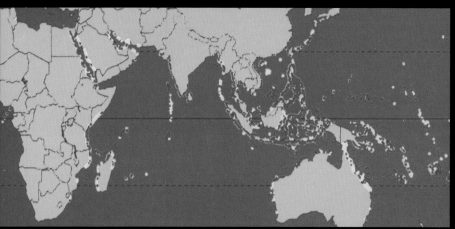

Map of endangered coral reefs. The red areas, equal to 27% of the total number of reefs, are at high risk, and the yellow ones at medium risk

It is estimated that there are now over 15 million scuba divers in the world

The increase in coastal development harms the growth of the coral reefs

Species), has been entered into by governments to protect them and to ensure their survival. While time allows the reefs to rectify the harm caused by natural phenomena, it worsens the damage inflicted by human-related phenomena and man's increasingly rapid progress. Everyone must make a commitment to ensuring that human activities and the development of protected areas are managed more efficiently, if the coral reefs that have existed on our planet for millions of years are to survive.

Signs of human activity are increasingly evident on the coral reefs

causing serious damage to the ecosystem of the coral reefs since it drives a market that, each year, deprives the reef ecosystems of at least 20 million fishes belonging to over 1,000 different species, and of over approximately 1,500 tons of madrepore. Many species such as sea turtles and dugongs are now endangered and an international agreement, the CITES (*Convention on International Trade in Endangered*

number of hotel rooms available has risen from 600 in 1988 to 16,000 in 1999. At sites frequented by scuba divers the area of damaged reef has been known to rise from 4% (percentage of degradation resulting from natural causes) to a maximum of 23%. The popularity of aquariums – there is now a total of at least 2 million enthusiasts in the world – is also

Coral reefs
are fragile structures:
we must respect them
to pass them on
to future generations

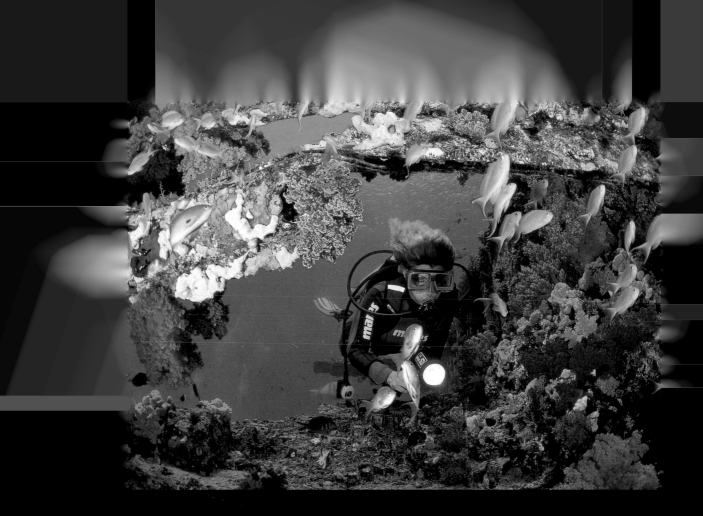

BIBLIOGRAPHY

Chicurel, **A.**, **Lagny**, **L.**, *Sinaï - Visions de plongeurs en Mer Rouge*, Paris, 2003. **Debelius**, **H.**, *Red Sea Reef Guide*, Frankfurt, 1998. **Harrison**, **P.**, **Misiewicz**, **A.**, *Reef Fishes and Corals of the Red Sea*, London, 2000. **Mojetta**, **A.**, **Ghisotti**, **A.**, *Pesci e coralli del Mar Rosso*, Milano, 1996. **Randall**, **J.E.**, *Sharks of Arabia*, London, 1986. **Randall**, **J.E.**, *Red Sea Reef Fishes*, London, 1983. **Sheppard**, **C.**, **Price**, **A.**, **Roberts**, **C.**, *Marine Ecology of the Arabian Region*, London, 1992. **Siliotti**, **A.**, *Sharm el-Sheikh Diving Guide*, Cairo, 1999. **Siliotti**, **A.**, *Pesci del Mar Rosso*, Verona, 2002.

PHOTOGRAPHIC CREDITS

DRAWINGS